*

Asceticism – an Analysis

(A Study of Hindu *Sanyāsam*)

*

Dr. Ramamurthy N.

M.Sc., B.G.L., CAIIB, CCP, DSADP, CISA, PMP, CGBL, Ph.D.

*

*

Title: Asceticism – an Analysis
(A Study of Hindu *Sanyāsam*)

First Edition: 2020

Author: **Dr. Ramamurthy N,**
http://ramamurthy.jāgruti.co.in/

Number of pages: 141

ISBN (13): 978-93-82237-67-9

Price: ₹ 200

*****

Table of Contents

*****

Dedication

Āchārya Devo Bhava

This book is dedicated to all the *Gurus* who bless, admonish, teach and uplift our charity and take us to achive the Moksha, the liberation. Let us seek their complete blessings to all.

Dr. Ramamurthy N.

*****

*****

SRI JAYADURGAYAI NAMAHA STD : 0431

SRIMATH POOJYA GURU PRANAVANANDHA SWAMIGAL
SRIVIDYA MAHA SOWBHAGYA PARAMBIKA PEETAM

SRI JAYADURGA SAPARYA SAMAJAM TRUST
ANDANALLUR (POST) TRICHY - 639 101.

Blessings – 1

श्री:

The Maharishis have given us the four types of Parama-Purushartas for the people of the world, namely the Ordinary Dharma, Special Dharma, Human Dharma, Raja Dharma, Purusha Dharma, Stree Dharma, Varna Dharma, Ashram Dharma, etc., inflicted.

We as human beings were created for these virtues to continue to take place. We must study the shastras in order to live like our ancestors with secular studies. Knowing so will make it easier for us to engage in virtues and to adhere to our own virtues. In the families, they live in the stages of Brahmacharyam, Gruhastam, Vanaprastam and Sannyasa and practice Dharma. This book will be very helpful in informing everyone about the ancient scientific virtues in this time when those traditions are declining a little.

What is asceticism in this age of declining scientific training due to circumstances? How many types are there? I am very happy to know that Dr. Ramamurthy has read and analyzed various books and many other sources and have come out with this book so that everyone can understand the qualifications, rituals etc. to receive it. So glad. We pray for the perfect grace and blessings of the Almighty Srividya Lalita Para Shodashi Devi for him and her family and all who read this.

Everyone should read and understand this book and attain Guru above the age of 65, learn Advaita Shastra and attain Moksha by following the Sannyasa Dharma. We also pray to all our Gurus, Srividya Mahasabhagya Para-Shodashi Devi and Sri Bhuvaneshwari Devi for the benefit of all.

Ahimsa Truth Bliss Auspicious

*****

Blessings – 2

'Jai Sri Mouna Guru'
SRI MOUNANDA TAPOVANAM
SRI SOWBHAGYA BHUWANESWARI PEETAM
D.No : 50-53-11/4, MIG-3, Seethammadhara North Extn.
Visakhapatnam, Andhra Pradesh-530013
Ph: +91-9963532728, Email : rajasimham123@gmail.com

Sri Gurubhyo Nama:

Sanyasa Dharma

வேண்டினுண் டாகத் துறக்க துறந்தபின்
ஈண்டியற் பால பல. Tirukkural 342

'Renunciation' made- ev'n here true pleasures men acquire;
'Renounce' while time is yet, if to those pleasures you aspire.

Dr. Ramamurthy N., has written very clearly and beautifully in detail about Sanyasa Dharma, according to Shastras and Upanishats, after doing lots of research.

The life span of a human being is divided into four parts. They are, Brahmacharyam (bachelor), Grahastam (married life), Vana Prastam (preparatory to sanyasam) and Asceticism.

The author has beautiful presentated, the first stage before the Sannyasa Ashram as chanting of Gayatri Japam in the Brahmacharya Ashram and other rituals, eternal Agni Hotram, eternal Karmanushtanas, etc., from the first day of the Sannyasa Ashram. From this first stage it is easy to go straight to the Sannyasa Ashram. This is one way.

After marriage the wife goes on the path of life with the people with dharma practices. This is followed by abstinence from the family bond. From this it is a condition to obtain the next permanent asceticism. The present day Sannyasa Dharma was started by Lord Sri Adi Shankara.

He has clearly stated how a Sanyasi has to be and what dharmas to perform. The author has mentioned in detail about the types of Sannyasa as there are many types of Sannyasa such as Thandi Sannyasi, Avadhuta Sannyasi and Sadhus.

It has been elaborated on Sannyasa Dharma in Hindu Dharma about what many Rishis and greats have mentioned. Sri Adi Shankara gave Sanyasam to his four primary disciples and established four mutts. These mutts act as roots to the tree of Hindu Dharma. The details about these mutts, the worship methods followed by all have been very clearly elaborated.

The sanyasa ashrama prescribed by Sri Adi Shankara has been followed by various great persons. Other acharyas like Sri Ramanujar, Ragavendrar, Ramakrishan Paramahamsa, Swami Vivekananda and all have quoted at the appropriate places. Kanchi Paramacharya, called as mobile living God by all, lived a century as per the dharma prescribed for Sanyasis. He has been quoted in most of the places.

Dr. Ramamurthy N, has the complete compassion of all the gurus, eleders and his parents. We pray with our presiding deity Mata Bhuvaneshwari to bless him, to continue his spiritual pursuit. We are happy that we have a role in this.

Let the service to God grow. Let the spirituality grow.

Dharma always wins.

Loka: Samasta: Sukhino Bhavantu

Narayana Narayana Narayana

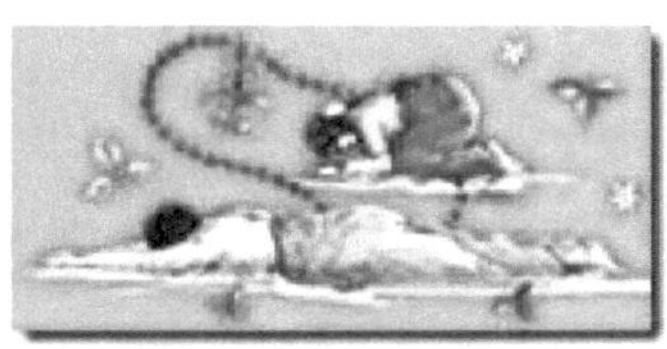

*****

Introduction

ॐ श्री गुरुभ्यो नमः । *Oṃ Śrī Gurubhyo Namaḥ* ।

गुरुर्ब्रह्मा गुरुर्विष्णु: गुरुर्देवो महेश्वरः । गुरु साक्षात् परं ब्रह्म तस्मै श्रीगुरवे नमः ॥
Gururbrahma Gururviṣṇuḥ Gururdevo Maheśvaraḥ ।
Guru Sākśāt Parabrahma Tasmai Śrīgurave Namaḥ ॥

गुरुवे सर्वलोकानां भिषजे भवरोगिनां । निधये सर्व विद्यानां दक्षिणा मूर्तये नमः ॥
Guruve Sarvloksansam Bhiṣaje Bhavaroginām ।
Nidhaye Sarva Vidhyānām Dakśiṇa Mūrtaye Namaḥ ॥

सदाशिव समारंभां शङ्कराचार्य मध्यमां। अस्मद आचार्य पर्यन्तां वन्दे गुरु परंपराम्
Sadāshiva Samārambām Śankarāchārya Madhyamām ।
Asmad Achārya Paranthām Vande Guru Paramparām ॥

श्रुति स्मृति पुराणानामालयं करुणालयम् । नमामि भगवत्पादंशंकरं लोकशंकरम्
Śruti Smruti Purānānām Ālayam Karunālayam ।
Namāmi Bhagavatapādam Śankaram Lokaśankaram ॥

वागर्थाविव सम्प्रुक्तौ वागर्थ प्रतिपत्तये । जगतः पितरौ वन्दे पार्वती परमेश्वरौ ॥
Vāgarthāviva Sampruktakou Vāgartha Pratipaye ।
Jagataḥ Pitarou Vande Pārvati Parameśwarou ॥

Our humble *pranams* to all our *Gurus*.

We hear and come across various terms like Rishi, Muni, Yogi, Siddha, Sadhu, Sanyasi, Yathi, Ascetic, Pakkiri, Swamiji, Madadhipathi, Jeeyar, Paramahamsar, Chaitanya, Agori and so on. Some have dressed up in saffron. Some people dress in different colors such as white, light saffron, red, green, yellow, blue, etc. Some people even do not dress up. Some people have tonsured[1] their heads, but some have *jada* hair and

[1] 280th Tirukkural – *"மழித்தலும் நீட்டலும் வேண்டா, உலகம் பழித்தது ஒழித்து விடின்"* – is worth comparable at this juncture – this means – No need to tonsure the head neither need to have a long hair, if got rid of all that have been accused by the world.

beard. Some have a stick in their hand, some have three sticks and some do not have any stick. They have a small cloth tied at the tip of the stick. What are all these? What are the differences? All these words denote the same people?

Such confusions and doubts may be in everyone's mind. This book is meant to get a clarity to all these.

Further, what do the Shastras prescribe for the *Sanyasi*s to live? During the Kali period, what changes have been made in terms of periodic national change?

Can women become ascetic – Some are called as *Swaminis* – Are they ascetics? Can a couple become *Sanyasi*? Can they live as couple even after getting *Sanyasam*? Let us try to discuss and get some clarifications for all these.

Whatever is mentioned in this book as duties or rules, etc., are all from Dharma Sutras and the result of discussions with various of serious *Sanyasi*s/ Swamiji. Nothing is the personal/ own opinion of the author. For this purpose, the author might have discussed with at least ten Swamijis.

Specifically, most of the inputs for the book were given by Ayyarmalai Pujayasri Pranavananda Swamiji and Tiruvannamalai Pujayashri Paramahamsananda Saraswathi Swamiji. Out humble pranams are due to them both.

Generally, it is very difficult to read Samskruta words in English with proper pronunciation. It is apt to read them in Samskruta script itself. But to benefit those who cannot read Samskruta script the *mantras* have been given in English also. The Samskruta words, when transliterated in English are denoted in *italics*. Normally diacritical marks will be used for transliteration of Samskruta words into English. But general readers are not fully conversant with diacritical marks and hence they find it difficult to read. Hence, it not been used in this book in normal texts. But for proper pronunciation it has been used in *mantras* and in some words.

Humble *pranams* are due to *Pujyasri Pranavananda Swamiji* of Ayyarmalai, who has given his blessings and some pleasantries about the author and the book.

Hearty thanks to all the good-hearted souls who enabled this book to be presented in this fashion. Attempts have been made to give this book as much error free as possible. Still if there are any errors, apologies are sought. If the errors are given as feedback, it will the next edition to be fault free.

There is no doubt that all the *Gurus* will shower their full c*om*passion and blessings to all those who read this book.

This book has also been published in in Tamil language simultaneously by the same author.

Chennai
2020 **Dr. Ramamurthy N.**

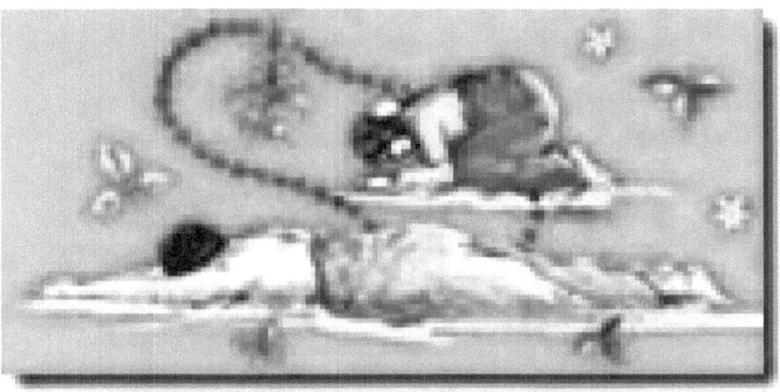

*****

Some Important Understandings

Before going into the main subject of this book, let us understand some of the key terms.

If we try to picturize the origin of this universe as stated in *Brahadaranyaka Upanishat* it will look as;

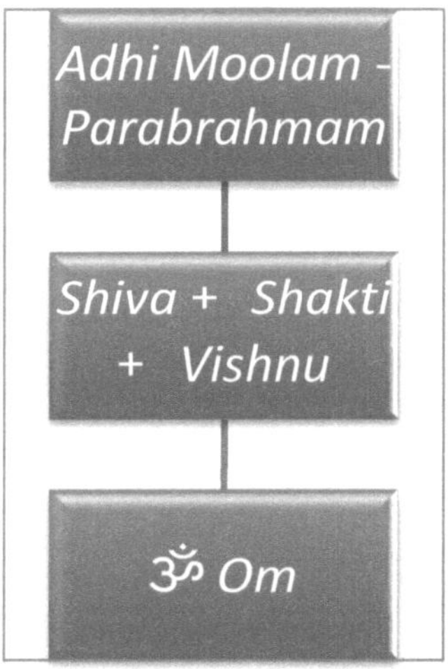

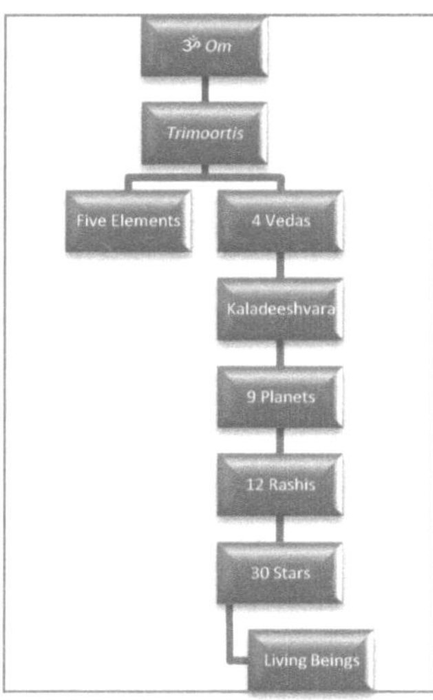

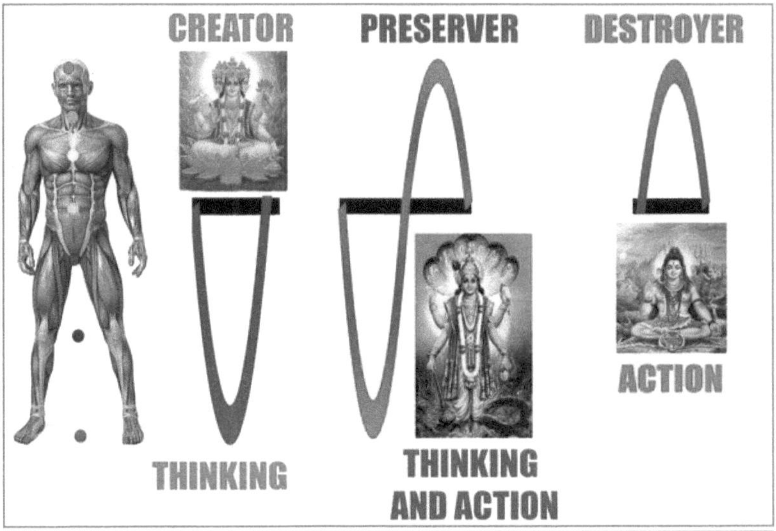
CREATOR
PRESERVER
DESTROYER
ACTION
THINKING
THINKING
AND ACTION

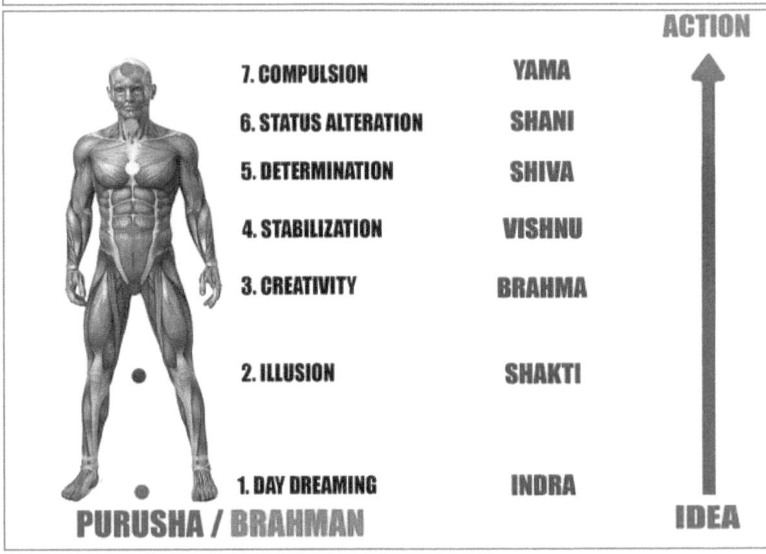
ACTION
7. COMPULSION
YAMA
6. STATUS ALTERATION
SHANI
5. DETERMINATION
SHIVA
4. STABILIZATION
VISHNU
3. CREATIVITY
BRAHMA
2. ILLUSION
SHAKTI
1. DAY DREAMING
INDRA
PURUSHA / BRAHMAN
IDEA

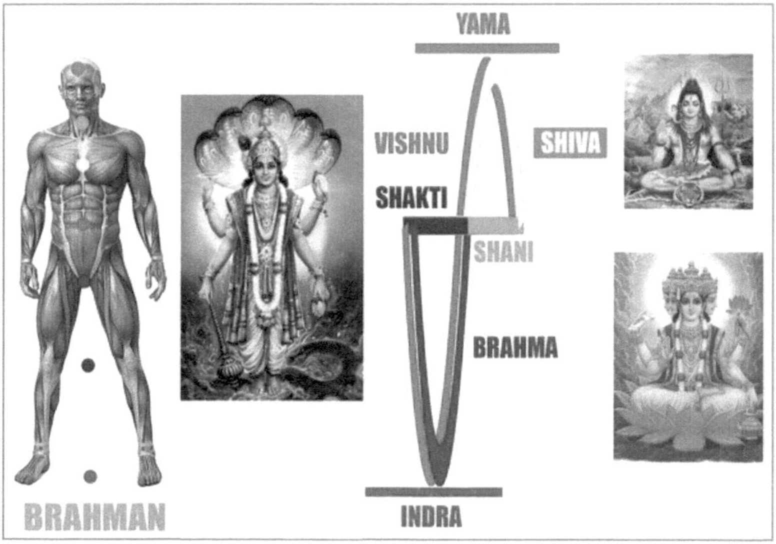
YAMA
VISHNU
SHIVA
SHAKTI
SHANI
BRAHMA
BRAHMAN
INDRA

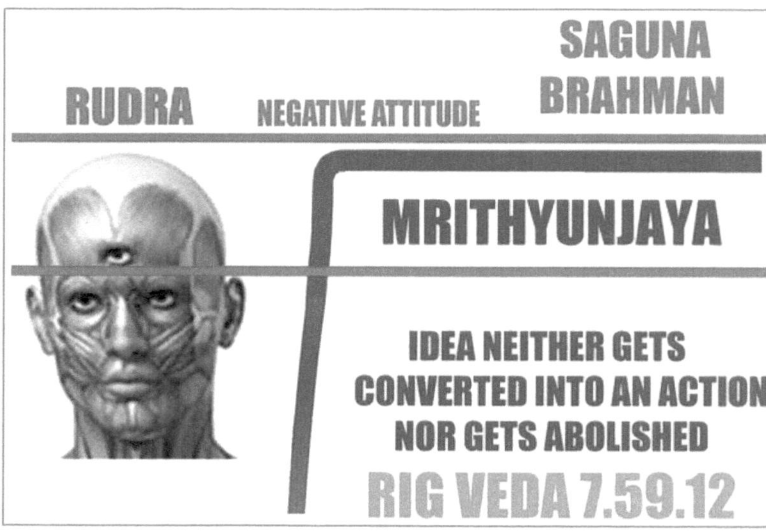
SAGUNA
BRAHMAN
RUDRA
NEGATIVE ATTITUDE
MRITHYUNJAYA
IDEA NEITHER GETS
CONVERTED INTO AN ACTION
NOR GETS ABOLISHED
RIG VEDA 7.59.12

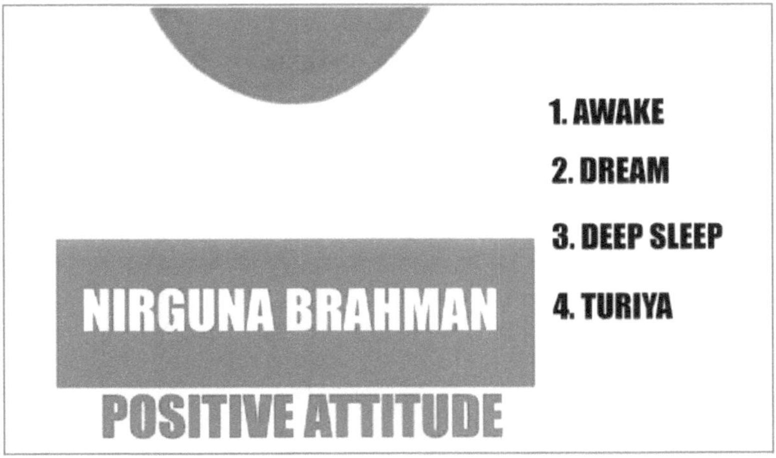

The *Aadhi Moolam*, also called as *Parabrahmam* or *Paramporul*, does not have any form or qualities. It does not fit within any limitations. However, in order to realize that *Brahmam* without any form, a sort of image worship is suggested. Once the maturity (*Saaloka*, *Saameepya* and *Saayujya*) is reached, there is no need for any restrictions and prescriptions to worship gods with different images, fasting, etc. Various *karmas* have to be performed to take us to that yogic position.

Rishi – A *Rishi* is a person who has wisdom, can call upon the deity, has spiritual knowledge and is able to control his senses.

After the *Maha Pralaya* (complete dissolution), *Brahmadeva* embarked on the creation of world. As a first step he created seven *Rishis* from his mind and continued human creation through them. Those seven *Rishis* are;

According to *Jaiminīya Brāhmaṇam* (2.218-221) the seven *rishis* are – Agastya, Atri, Bharadwājar, Goutamar, Jamadagni, Vaśişţar and Viśwāmitra.

According to *Brahadaranyaka Upanishat* (2.2.6) the seven *rishis* are – Śāṇdilyar, Atri, Bharadwājar, Goutamar, Jamadagni, Vaśişţar and Viśwāmitra.

According to *Gopata Brāhmaṇam* (1.2.8), of later years the seven *rishis* are – Kāśyapar, Brugu, Bharadwājar, Goutamar, Jamadagni, Vaśiştar and Viśwāmitra.

Indian names of the stars of Sapta Rishi

According to Shrimad Bhagavatam (8.13.5), the Rishis change in every Manvantara. *Shastras* say that the earlier Rishis shine in the sky in the form of a star. The Sapta Rishi zone is near the pole star in the sky. The Seven Rishis and their Wives in the present Vaivasvata Manvantaram; Atri (Anusuya), Brugu (Puloma), Gutsa, Vaśiştar (Arundhati), Goutamar (Akalya), Kāśyapar (Titi & Atiti) and Angīrasar (Suruoā).

In the daily *Sandhyavandana* also, the names of these seven Rishis are being announced. These Rishis are our first ancestors we call them as our Gotram.

The Vedic *mantras* have manifested themselves to the Rishis by intuition. That is why the Rishis came to be known as the *Mantradrashtaa*. It is customary of every chanter to announce the names of the respective Rishis during the chanting of the mantras.

Munis – A term referring to ancient Indian monks or ancient Indian saints. Sages know the truth, not based on scientific texts but through self-realization. For instance, let us consider Veda Vyasa. He is called as Vyasa Muni – he has realized the complete of Vedas and has divided it into four and offered to us for the benefits of the entire world.

The word *'Muni'* is derived from the Samskruta root-verb (धातु), *'manan'*. *Manan* means to think. A *Muni* is an introspecting (अन्तर्दर्शन) or thoughtful person.

According to *Shrimad Vishnu Bhagavatam* – a *Muni* is an expert in mental-speculation or thought (remember मनन) or perception.

According to the *Shrimad Bhagavad Gita* (2.56) – a *Muni* is the one who can stimulate the mind in a variety of ways for mental assumptions, without coming up with a factual explanation. Where does this mental speculation come from? Through intuition (अन्तर्दर्शन – Inward looking – Introspection).

"*Mounam Aacarati Iti Munih* – मौनं आचरति इति मुनिः" – One who observes the fast of silence to prevent distraction during the penance is called as *Muni*.

A *Rishi* is a title given to one who knows all about the Sastras and the science behind it.

That is why the sentences spoken by Rishis are considered very true "आर्ष वाक्य". There is a Tamil saying as "Rishi Wakko – ரிஷி வாக்கோ".

Yogi – One who is dived into the worldly enjoyments is called *'Bhogi'*. Against this, the person who has sacrificed any type of enjoyment is a 'yogi'. A *yogi* is a practitioner of yoga, which was started by sage Patanjali. Its feminine is called Yogini.

84 MahaSiddhas

Siddhar – Who can be called as Siddhar? One who has attained Siddhi is a Siddhar. The term Siddhi, nowadays, means death. That is not correct. The elders say that "power, valor, strength and extraordinary ability" is the supernatural, supernatural, power of is called Siddhi. But it is treated as a game of wits.

Usually these are eight Siddhis (Ashta Maasiddhi). They are;

1. Aṇimā: the ability to become smaller than the smallest, reducing one's body to the size of an atom or even become invisible.
2. Mahimā: the ability to become infinitely large, expanding one's body to an infinitely large size.

3. Laghimā: the ability to become weightless or lighter than air.
4. Prāpti: the ability to instantaneously travel or be anywhere at will.
5. Prākāmya: the ability to achieve or realize whatever one desires.
6. Īśiṭva: the ability to control nature, individuals, organisms, etc. Supremacy over nature and ability to force influence upon anyone.
7. Vaśiṭva: the ability to control all material elements or natural forces.

The eighth is given as either:

8. *Kāma-avasayitva* (per *Kṣemarāja* and *Vyasa*): satisfaction, suppression of desire, or (as Yatrakāmāvasāyitva) wishes coming true.

   Or

   Garimā (per the Rāmānanda Sampradāya): the ability to become infinitely heavy and be immovable by anyone or anything.

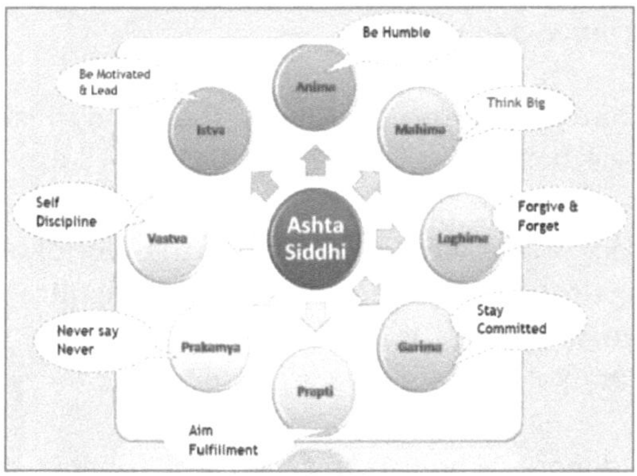

A siddha is a person who is an expert in one or more of the above 8. In Ramayana, it has been mentioned that Sri Anjaneya was an expert in all the 8 siddhis. Shrimad Bhagavatam (11-15) chapter explains about all these 8 siddhis

<u>*Sadhu*</u> – Males are called Sadhu and females are called Saadhvi or Saadhwinee. A religious *sanyasi*, who eats through begging alms, a holy person in religion, who renounces the worldly enjoyments, is called as a Sadhu. They are sometimes referred to as *Jogi*, *Sanyasi* or *Vairagi*.

Sadhu means a serious follower of Sadhana (practice) or the path of spiritual discipline. Although most of the sadhus are yogis, not all yogis are sadhus. The Sadhus devote themselves to attaining the fourth and final state of asceticism, moksha (liberation) through meditation and contemplation.

The sadhus often wear simple clothes. Saffron colored garments in Hinduism, white or none in Jainism. It symbolizes their asceticism. A Sadhvi in Hinduism and Jainism, sometimes called Aryika.

In short, the words *sanyasi*, *sadhu* or *yati* are all treated as one and the same in this book. All those who are serene are all Sadhus. Are we not saying that the man who sits peacefully as sitting as a Sadhu in our routine?

The terms *Sanyasi*, saint, Pakkiri, etc., denote the same. This is how a *sanyasi* is called. Colloquially they are called as Swamiji. Is it not a respectable way to call?

Matathipati – Head of a mutt – The monastery is known as a *Matathipati*, as long as, he is in charge of it and performing puja rituals.

Jeeyar – A *Vaishnava Sanyasi*, worshipping Lord *Vishnu*, is called a *Jeeyar*.

Chaitanya – A person who decides to lead whole of his life as a bachelor is called as Chaitanya. This has been discussed in detail in a later chapter.

Paramahamsar – The Samskruta word *Paramahamsar* (परमहंस) is a, Religious-theology related title. This applies to enlightened Hindu spiritual teachers. Meaning "Supreme Hamsa". It refers to spiritual discrimination. The Hamsa is equal in land and in the water. Likewise, the true Paramahamsar views all worldly affairs equally. Being in divine ecstasy and simultaneously awakening is paramount status; The "royal Hamsa" of the soul floats in the cosmic ocean, whose body and sea are the manifestations of the same Brahmam.

The word 'Paramahamsa' refers to a person who is awake everywhere in all the times. Paramahamsa is the highest level of spiritual growth the ultimate realist in this is the Paramahamsa *Sanyasi*. One example known to all of us is Ramakrishna Paramahamsar. He was not formally initiated into *Sannyasa*. He was a Married Grahastar. However, he is considered more than any Swamiji. The state of the Paramahamsa asceticism of a *sanyasi* is discussed in detail in different chapters.

Agori – Agori is a South Based (*Vamaachara*) *sanyasi* – A small group of *Shaivas*. They perform funeral ritual rites. They often live in cremation grounds. They coat the burial ashes on the body and shape the bones from human bodies – skulls (skulls) into jewelry. Their practices may sometimes contradict orthodox Hinduism ritual.

Many Agori priests are highly respected by the rural people. This is because of their intense erection rituals and abstinence and wrong practices and they have healing powers through penance and sacrifices. Even in the extreme cold – like the Kailash Mountain – they roam around, just flushing ashes around the body with nothing else as dress.

Gurujis – For a person who is unhappy or not satisfied in life, the *guru* act as a guide and lead him through a good life.

Upaasakas – Sri Adi Shankara himself has defined an *Upasaka* – that one who selects one of the *Shanmadhas*, treat the same as the universal *Shakti* – Parabrahmam, is the *Upasaka*.

Baabaa – *Baba* is an honorable term of Persian origin. It is used in India and many West Asian and South Asian cultures. It is used as a prefix or suffix for their names, referring to Hindu and Sikh *sanyasi*, a mark of respect. An example known to all of us is Sai Baba.

Baba is a title conferred on the head of a particular order of Sufi saints, like Babi Bulle Shah and Rehman Baba. The word is also accepted in Malaysia as a word of honor to invite Chinese people born in the British Strait settlement. Baba is a familiar word for 'father' in many languages. In India, it has even been modified for addressing male children.

Sadhus and *Sannya*sins

Every religion has a band of anchorites who lead the life of seclusion and meditation. There are Bhikkhus in Buddhism, Fakirs in Islam, Fakirs in Sufism and Fathers and Reverends in Christianity. The glory of a religion will be lost absolutely if you remove these hermits or *Sannya*sins or those who lead a life of renunciation and divine contemplation. It is these people who maintain or preserve the religions of the world. It is these people who give solace to the householders when they are in trouble and distress. They are the messengers of the Atman-knowledge and heavenly peace. They are the harbingers of divine wisdom and peace. They are the disseminators of spiritual knowledge and *Upanishatic* revelations. They heal the sick, comfort the forlorn and nurse the bedridden. They bring hope to the hopeless, joy to the depressed, strength to the weak and courage to the timid, by imparting the knowledge of the Vedanta and the significance of the *"Tat Tvam Asi" Mahavakya*.

It has been tried to understand some concepts/ jargons mentioned in the Introduction chapter. We will further try to answer some queries raised in that chapter.

*****

Āśramas

Our *vedas*, *smritis*, scriptures, etc., have formulated about *ashrams* and the methods to follow. Depending on the growth of the mind and body of the human being, the lifecycle is divided into 4 *ashramas* and the lifestyles of each *ashrama* are prescribed as below:

1. *Brahmacharyam*
2. *Grahastāsramam – gārhastyam*
3. *Vānaprastam*
4. *Sanyāsam*

1. ***Brahmacharyam*** – *Brahmacharyam* is meant for studying/ learning education. Immediately after *upanayanam*, the *guru* takes him to the school (*gurukul*). But nowadays, the admission in schools has to be sought even before the birth of the baby and on account of various family issues; the baby has to be sent to school before even completion of 3 years of age. However, it is requested to perform the *upanayanam* at the appropriate age.

2. ***Grahastāsramam*** – The boy has to marry a girl suitable to him in qualities and beauty, with the permission of the parents and with the blessings of elders. He procreates virtuous babies through her and faithfully does the duties due to *Devas*, *pitrus*, friends and relatives. This is the main aim of this *āshrama*.

3. ***Vānaprastam*** – This *ashrama* is meant to handover the family responsibilities to the children and migrate to a lonely place like a forest alongwith wife and lead a simple life always thinking of divine matters. This *āshrama* is meant for maturity of the mind and preparing oneself to the next *āshrama*.

4. ***Sanyāsam*** – At this juncture, the individual has to renounce everything like the assets, wife, children, etc. and should not keep anything for the self. He has to beg for alms and eat only once a day – just to keep the body alive. He also should not continue to stay in any particular place for more than one night. His thought should

always be on Godly matters and he has to advise and initiate others on divinity.

Shrimad Bhagavatam (3-12-42 & 43) explains these *ashrama*-s.

Note: the sage *Āpastamba*, who globalized the *vaidheeka* procedures, has categorically indicated that *Vānaprasta āshrama* need not be applied to this era (*kali yuga*). It is enough if people follow the other three *āshramas*.

Among all the four *āshramas* defined above, the *grahastāsrama* is in the higher plane. Sages have given two main reasons for the same:

- Only a *grahastan* can feed and protect the other two viz., *brahmachāri* and *sanyasi*. He only has that right and duty. The other two cannot cook on their own.
- Again, only a *grahastan* has a right to procreate virtuous children and protect the *dharma* of this world. The other two are ineligible for this purpose.

Hence the *grahastāsrama*, which is so highly treated among all the 4, has to settle itself well. It is not only meant to satiate the sensual wishes. It is for the welfare of the entire world including *devas, pitrus* and others.

Let everyone fulfill their obligations relating to their *ashrama* and enlighten the world with Bliss.

Four Ashrams of Vedic Life

Sanyāsa Āśramam

Sannyasa (*saṃnyāsa*) is the life stage of renunciation within the Hindu philosophy of four-based life stages known as ashramas. *Sannyasa* is traditionally conceptualized for men in late years of their life, but young *brahmacharis* have had the choice to skip the householder and retirement stages, renounce worldly and materialistic pursuits and dedicate their lives to spiritual pursuits.

Sannyasa is a form of asceticism, is marked by renunciation of material desires and prejudices, represented by a state of disinterest and detachment from material life and has the purpose of spending one's life in peaceful, love-inspired, simple spiritual life. An individual in *Sannyasa* is known as a *Sanyas*i in Hinduism, which in many ways parallel to the Sadhu traditions of Jain monasticism, the bhikkhus of Buddhism and the monk traditions of Christianity.

Sannyasa has historically been a stage of renunciation, ahimsa (non-violence) peaceful and simple life and spiritual pursuit in Indian traditions.

Literature, to them, means a favour or a spiritual discipline. Although most of the sadhus are yogis, not all yogis are sadhus. A sadhu is a slowly liberating person, the fourth and final *ashramam*. His goal is to attainment of Brahmam through life, meditation and contemplation. The Sadhus often wear simple clothes, the saffron dress in Hinduism, the Jain religion is white, sometimes nothing and their asceticism denotes worldly possessions.

The word sadhu appears in the *Rig* and *Atharva Veda* scriptures to mean "straight to the goal". In Brahman's plots of Vedic literature, the word refers to a well-adjusted kind, willing, efficient or peaceful, secure, good, virtuous, honorable, just and noble. In mythology, the word is mentioned as a holy, holy man, virtuous, upright or perfect.

In the Samskrutam, the Sadhu (good man) does not care about their own spiritual practices. This refers to the revivalists who chose to live for other lives sake and caring the society as a whole.

In Samskrutam, the word *'Saadhu'* comes from the root word *'sad'*. It means "to reach one's goal", or 'straight' or "increase in power". Same word *'saadhana'* means spiritual practice. This means practicing spiritual discipline.

Today, there could be around 4 to 5 lakhs of *sanyasi*s in India. They are widely respected for their sanctity. It is also thought that the sadhustic practices of the Sadhus help to burn a large part of their karma and of the society. They feel that this is beneficial to the community. Hence, donations are received from many people as they are considered beneficial to the society.

A few *sanyasi*s are naked and they are called Digambar, who cover their bodies with their hair called 'braids'. They are involved in various religious rituals. Some prefer solo meditation, others like chanting or meditation and a few group prayers. They usually live a simple life, with very little possessions or food and drinks obtained through donations from others. Many sadhus have rules for collecting objects and never return to the same place not to disturb the residents. They usually have to walk to distant places. They are homeless and travel to temples and pilgrimage centers as part of their spiritual practice.

Shaiva Sadhus are devotees to Lord Shiva. Vaishnava sadhus are devotees to Lord Vishnu or His incarnation like Rama and Krishna. Vaishnava sadhus are sometimes called *vairagis*. Shakta sadhus are very few in number.

These general divisions are represented by various subdivisions, different philosophies, philosophical schools and traditions. The philosophy is a necessity as far as the Bharat Sanatana Dharma is concerned. For others, it is an entertainment (philosophy is a pastime).

The four sages viz., Sanakar, Sanantanar, Sanatkumaarar and Sanaatanar were born from the mind of Lord Brahma (*Maanasa Putras*). They refused to enter into the worldly life of *Pravruti Margham* or and entered the path of asceticism. All the four sons were the forerunners of the *Sannyasa* path. Sri Dattatreya was also one of the original *Sanyasi*s.

The *Sanyas*is of today are the descendants of Dattatreya or Sri Adi Shankara or the above four sons.

In a nutshell, *Sannyasa* is the act of renouncing material life to pursue a spiritual life. A *Sanyasi/ Sanyasi* (m) *Sanyas*ini (f) is a person who renounces, a renunciate, an ascetic, a monk/ nun and so on.

Kanchi Paramacharya says about asceticism – our religion dictates that all human beings should at one time or other come to the state of asceticism. That does not mean everyone has to give up on themselves right now. That will automatically depart from us in one or other birth. It happens naturally if one lives as per Dharma rules with faith in God.

The *Maha Mrutyunjaya mantra* in Veda –

ॐ त्र्यम्बकं यजामहे सुगन्धिं पुष्टिवर्धनम् । उर्वारुकमिव बन्धनान् मृत्योर्मुक्षीय मामृतात् ॥

Om Trayambakam Yajāmahē Sugantim Puṣṭivardhaṉam I
Urvārukamiva Bandhaṉāṉ Mrutyōrmukṣīya Māmrutāt II

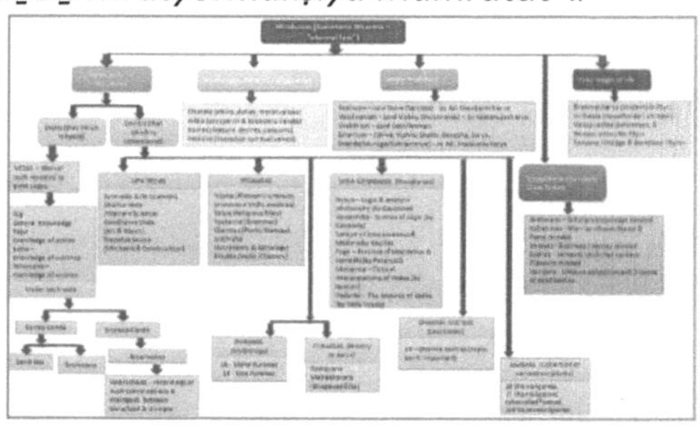

Just as the cucumber fruit is freed from the vine, so must the bondage of life should be freed. Cucumber creeper will spread on the ground. Therefore, it is not possible for the fruti to move after it is ripe. The wine will remove itself and release from the nipple.

Shrimad Bhagavatam 11-19-37 & 38 chapters say – It is good to be free from karmas, but, completly leaving the karmas is asceticism.

Similarly, the affections that surround the soul will automatically recede in order for it to remain so. One has to wait for the right time – the mind to ripe – to mature. Then man automatically attains the state of enlightenment. The sages do not need to let go of the bond. The affections of the sages will naturally depart from them. It is enough to surrender to God and wait for wisdom to attain.

*****

Tools for Liberation

In this book we find and see and we are going to read many things such as *Swayam*, self-knowledge and so on. What do they mean?

The Vedas say many sentences – *Praghnānam Brahma, Aham Brahmāsmi, Tatvamasi, Ayatmā Brahma, Ekam Brahma...* – what are these?

Only one answer to all these – i.e. self-realization. Self is *brahmam* and *brahmam* is self. Realizing the *advaita* philosophy that both are same. This has to be realized by self and cannot be explained in writing.

If someone says that sugar is sweet, the hearer understands it in one way. The same person understands it differently when he tastes the sugar in his tongue. Then only he can enjoy and appreciate himself. Similarly, one can understand and appreciate the whole self, only by self-knowing. That is the very purpose of *Sannyasa* Dharma.

1. *Swayam* – Looking at us if someone asks "Who are you?", we will reply 'I', which is the state of mind, intellect and the five senses. Normally in the eyes of the world this may seem the perfect reply. Actually, this is not correct. The *Upanishat*s claim that "*Sat-Chit-Aanandam*" is our nature. It means that our nature is existence, is perfect knowledge. Even though our image is "*Sat-Chit-Aanandam*", we have thought of ourselves as non-physical body, mind, intellect and thoughts. This is the practice right from the beginning, the origin not known.

Our nature, we are searching for things that are physical, etc., which are not 'we'. 'Me' is forever – I was born one day and I hope to die one day and think that I know, I am the most knowledgeable, or goof or most intelligent.

Eternal blissful, boundless me, is thought as – I am the inferior, I am the saddest in the world. Eternal Pure Me, is thought as – I know whether I am Bobby or I am a saint. The Upanishats claim that the way we think of ourselves is the cause of all our own sorrow.

This body is like a shirt for the soul in it. After this birth and death, the soul takes off this old shirt and puts on another shirt (the new body). Thus, the life cycle is going on. This is aptly said as "Birth is not the beginning and death is not an end". Moksha is the state of stopping this life cycle and the soul not being born again.

For my existence, if I know myself as a soul with *Sat-Chit-Aanandam*, all my activities past-present-future efforts for knowledge and happiness will end.

The text "*Kaivalya Navaneetam*" says, for those who knows themselves there is no perversity. Knowing oneself is the way to permanently free oneself from all samsara bindings. There is no other option - *Purusha Sookhtam* says, "*Nāṉyaḥ Pantā VityatēSyaṉāya*".

2. <u>*Śravaṇam*</u> – Hearing – Hearing from the Guru – quietude – the lust to hear more and more from the Guru. The first hearing is to formally listen to the *Mahaavaakyaas* from the Guru. Hearing the *Prastaana Traya*[2] is to know the soul/ *Brahmam*. Apart from the Upanishats, which are supposed to give the soul knowledge with evidences, the direct knowledge (*Pratyaksham*), the assumption that the knowledge of the soul will not be helpful, must be upheld by the Guru. *Shrimad Bhagavad Gita* says that one should worship the Guru by doing services to him and get the self-knowledge.

Faith and confidence are the main things in hearing. The key to attaining enlightenment is the unwavering confidence placed in the Guru's *Vedanta* sentences.

Guru's advice is of three kinds – depending on the maturity of the disciples – the *Srishti Drushti* Argument, the *Drushti Srishti* Argument and the *Ajata* (unborn) Argument.

The *Srishti Drushti* Argument is meant for the disciples with lukewarm wisdom, less confidence and less *mumukshutvam*. This world is truly there. It is to begin with the idea that I am born, grow up and die in a

---

[2] The trio *Brahma Sootram, Upanishats* and *Srimad Bhagavad Gita* is called Prastaana Trayam. Some more details can be seen about this in other chapters.

state of insanity and gradually inquire and raise the mind of the sage and give the wisdom of the Advaita wisdom "all souls are one". More often, 90% of the Vedic rituals in the world belong to this category.

The second *Drushti Srishti* argument is for monogamous disciples. He who attains a moderate degree of achievement, who sees this world as equal to the dream, whoever knows that "there are sights just because of the One who sees," is taught by this method.

The third form is for those whoever achieves the quintessence of integrity – Whoever sees this world as equal to the dream, he knows that "there are sights only because of the one who sees". There is only one soul. There is no such thing as the world. (*Jaatha* means birth – *Ajaatha* means not born). It will be taught that there are no separate philosophies of soul and *Eswaran*. The same applies to the person, who is perfectly saturated with sages. This is what Sri Rama preaches to Hanuman as "the *Maandukyam* is enough" (माण्डूक्यं एकमेव अलम्).

The merits of pros and cons of the disciple determine the doctrine of subversion. This is a continuation of the spiritual achievements of the *Sadhakas* in the past. Hence, the argument that, Bhagavan Ramana Maharishi and Ramakrishna Paramahamsa did not perform any karmas *sadhanas* or they have learnt anything formally from any guru will not apply. They are exceptions. These is called as Outliers in Statistics. In Shrimad Bhagavad Gita, also Sri Krishna praises that "He who has wisdom at the end of many births attains to me".

Therefore, we need to know what is worthy of us and how much wisdom we have, etc. Without a high or low self-esteem, proper evaluation is very important to the Sadhana. The person who wants to hear the advice of a guru should necessarily have things like dharma, devotion to Guru, intelligence and philosophy.

3. *Mananam* – Thinking – Stirring what was heard – Moving on to think to get the doubts cleared. The philosophy of the mind is to remove the *Pratibhaksha* (counter-arguments) of the soul from the Guru's *Vedanta* arguments. The soul is a six-sided dimension-less. Only one – no two. Do such qualifications fit to us or not? It is to think and

apply the souls to Himself with the appropriate Veda sentences – that is called *Mananam*.

Poorva Paksha is very important in *mananam*. Faith and confidence were important in Shravanam. Similarly, asking questions and getting the doubts cleared is very important in *Mananam*. The Divine World in full of *Vyavahara* – this is not true in reality. This is ok and this is not – has to be decided on each and not-applicable things should be removed. And the soul must remain in the mind until it is over.

It is a real piracy that the soul is excluded from inquiring into – that is real *vairagya*. The completion of consciousness is the device of the mind. At the end of the mananam, only 'self' is left. All questions and thoughts are ended when all the subversions are gone.

4. *<u>Nididhyaasanam</u>* – sacrificing everything – *Nishtai* (meditation) – Continuous Soul Meditation. Unless *mananam* is completed, neither *Nididhyaasanam* nor *Advaita* knowledge can be achieved. Mananam is done perfectly, that is, to eliminate what is not good and to remain in Him alone. This is what is called soul meditation. Soul determination can be achieved through *Nididhyaasanam*.

"*Vipareeta Bhavana Nivruttiyartam Nididhyaasanam*" - For many births, the 'ego' possessed in this body, the knowledge of 'self' kept in the mind, will be habitually revealed to us. It is called cranky feeling. Only by removing it can the soul be sustained. Therefore, the spiritual meditation or *Nididhyaasanam* must be done. Therefore, with effort, the soul philosophy must be established in the intellect.

Mananam is 100 times better than hearing. *Nididhyaasanam* is one lakh times better than *Mananam*. Still, Meditation without an object (*Nirvikalpa Samadhi*) which leads to knowledge of consciousness, is limitlessly better.

The end of *nididhyaasanam* is to be grounded in the soul philosophy. It is called the *Nirvikalpa Samadhi*. That is the end.

In the text called *Sri Devi Bhagavatam*, the ten chapters from 31 to 40, in the 7th *Skanda* are called *Sri Devi Gita*[3]. In this Gita, verses 7-34-15 to 7-34-20, the *shravanam, mananam* and *nididhyaasanam* are being explained in her own words of *Sri Devi*.

5. <u>*Aatmaanubhava*</u> (Soul Experience) – The end of *Nididhyaasana* is the soul self-experience.

Sri Adi Shankarar also in his *Gita Bhashyam* (18.55) says that "The ultimate limit of soul wisdom is the soul determination (*atma nishtai*). The knowledge about self-experience is said to be the boundary of *nishtai*. Atma-related wisdom should not be tried to attain. *Naama-roopa* (Name-image) without soul things that are implanted in the soul should be done only by *Nivruti* (removal)".

The person who desires the knowledge of self or soul experience must first sacrifice everything. It is a life, a lifestyle of asceticism called *Nivruti* life style. Contemporary monasticism is found in mere clothing. The *Sanyasa*m seeking the Eesan, is a tool for moksha. Shastras also say the same thing. The *Brahadaranyaka Upanishat* (4.4.22) states - "*Putreshana, Vidheshana, Lokeshana*" – what will I do with my children, what will I do with this world... People for whom the soul is the world and all the saints who have been before, have sacrificed everything and lived by alms. *Katopanishat* (2.4.1) reveals – man is outward looking. Not seeing the *antharatma*. One who seeks the soul of *Pratyak* through inward looking, only sees the atma by reaching the status of undeath.

6. <u>*Jeevan Mukti* and *Videha Mukti*</u> – Self-realization and liberation from the body – Even though the purpose of the *Vedas* is to make every human to reach *Moksha*, not all men want *Moksha*. By seeing that every person in the world has various goals, the *Veda-mata*, with a motherly affection suggests different tools/ ways, considering her children's merits, desires and strategies to meet their needs and desires.

It is certain that the spirituality is clearly achieved by the *nirvikalpa samadhi* (deep meditation without wavering). It is the mind that is alien

---

[3] The author of this book has written separate books in English and Tamil on "*Sri Devi Gita*".

to it, the soul philosophy is mixed with the thoughts of the mind", says *Viveka Choodaamani*.

Eliminating foreign matters is very important for that purpose. Wisdom attained after the release from the samadhi does not deviate. He is the *Jeevan Muktan*. The *Mundaka Upanishat* states, "After seeing the *Paramatma*, the knots in the heart are shattered. All happiness is destroyed".

The mind of the wise person who attains the soul-experience, is in the level state. The wise people call this as Level Samadhi. It is the goal of *Jeevan Mukti*, which is to eradicate the ego *'Aham'* (I), fully from these *Stoola-Sookshma*[4] (subtle and physical) bodies. In the same way, the admiration of the three bodies can be overwhelming. Gita (3.17) states that after he is satisfied with the soul, "he has nothing else to do".

Mundaka Upanishat (3.2.9) states "One who realizes the *Brahmam*, becomes that *Brahmam* itself". Whatever adorable tasks he was performing before self-realization, he continues to do the same task after self-realization also without any affection to his body.

His body is suffering on account of the *praarabda karma* (sins of earlier births brought forward). Once the *praarabda karma* is exhausted, it is said by the wise men, the person attains *Videha Mukti*. The *Gnani* does not find any difference in this regard. In the eyes of others, this is meant to be understood for worldly affairs.

Briefly looking through an illustration picturestically;

The different steps or stage of *Atma* knowledge;

[4]*Stoola* means which can be seen by eyes and *Sookshma* means which cannot. If this can be compared to contemporary computer science – Stoola can be compared to hardware and Sookshma to software. Hardware can be seen by eyes and software cannot. However, only if both join together a computer system will work smoothly..

Following the rules prescribed by the one's own religion

The *karmas*/ activities done without any prejudice/ desire

Karma Sanyaasam

Knowledge obtained through a *Guru*.

Moksham – liberation – *Gnaana Nishtai*

7. *Brahma Darshanam* – witnessing the *Brahmam* – The entire text of *Eeshaavasya Upanishat* talks about the tools to reach *Moksham*. The first verse is;

> *Om Īśā Vāsyamidam Sarvam Yatkiñca Jakatyām Jagat* ।
> *Tēṉa Tyaktēṉa Bhuñjītā Mā Gṛutaḥ Kasyasviddhaṉam* ॥

All this is for habitation by the Lord, whatsoever is individual universe of movement in the universal motion. By that renounced thou should enjoy; lust not after any man's possession.

The first quartet "*Īśā Vāsyamitam Sarvam*" itself a great Veda sentence. This *Upanishat* is named after the very first sentence of this Upanishat. The knowledge that "everything is God" is what we see. This verse is told to the wise man who strives to attain enlightenment. This is the goal for all the *saadhakas*. All the tangible and immovable things we see in this world are incompatible with our experience. But all the *Upanishats* call this as *Brahmam*. Being a scripture, it cannot be ruled out also. Therefore, it is necessary to examine how all the things can be God. The third quartet of the *mantra* also outlines the guidelines.

The second quartet of the *mantra*, '*Jagatyam*' in the "*Yatkiñca Jakatyām Jagat*", means the world and the second, '*Jagat*', is the most immovable and moving in the earth. That is to say, all that we see in this world, is to be concealed by the wisdom of "all these things".

Shastras claim that all the objects in this world are *naama-roopa panchakam*. That is to say, the name (*naama*) - form (*roopa*) - *Sat-Chit-Aanandam* has all the five-parts here. Of these, *Sat-Chit-Aanandam* is the image of God. Is the source of everything. In fact, the self-image of the soul in the form of *Sat-Chit-Aanandam*, appears as a name form of unconsciousness. After learning the *Upanishats* from the *Guru*, then it should be got cleared that all the souls, all things are eternal, through the tactics told by *Shrutis*, that the myths are not real.

This is what is said, "Save yourself by sacrifice". We need to dismiss transient names. "*Jaayate Gachati Iti Jagat*" - is the disappearance of the world. This is the goal of this world. In this way, entire universe is transient. It would be impossible if the body, mind, intellect, senses and worldly objects that once appeared to be believed and maintained in order to be true. It is clear that these are mere forms and the soul forms the same form of the soul, by the soul vision. We must withdraw from the truth that we have been given to ourselves. This is what the *mantra* *"Īśā Vāsyamidam Sarvam"* says, "this is the truth".

The word *'Vāsyam'* in the *mantra* is derived from the root word which means "*Vasa-āchādane*" – means cover in closing. In *Shrimad Bhagavad Gita* (10.20), Lord *Shri Krishna* says, "I am the soul of all living beings" Again he says (13.02) and "I am the One who sees all the souls". He affirms (18.61), he and his *karma* are chased by illusion. "And the words such as "*Aham Brahmaasmi*", *'Tatvamasi'*, "*Pragnaanam Brahma*" and "*Ayamaatma Brahma*" refer to the unity of the two – *Jeeva* and *Eeshwara*. There is no difference between the two.

The second precept of this mantra - "*Tēṉa Tyaktēṉa Bhuñjītā*" - save you from that sacrifice. Amity is attained through sacrifice, not by *karma*, sons or by itself. *Shrimad Bhagavad Gita* (5.13) reads "Leave all the works of the mind".

The sooner a person conducts his life according to *Vedas*, the more he becomes aware that everything he does in *karma* is immutable. This is called Eternal-Transient wisdom. After this discernment, the desire to do anything for himself, as a duty imposed on him, services to god *Eshwar*. Naturally there is devotion to the Lord (*Saguna Brahma – Brahmam* with qualities). The outward gross rituals are diminished and the mind concentrates on subtle karmas like meditation. Then he renounces all the *karmas* and attains the Guru who is a *Brahma Nishta* and learns the *Upanishats* (*Vedanta*) and attains the soul wisdom. *Brahma-Nishtai* is complete with the *Shravanam* (learning) and *Mananam* (repeating). This is the end of *Samsara*.

These can be referred to as the *Naama-Roopa-Guna-Kriya*-caste-relationship over sound (*shabdas*). Even *Vedas* cannot explain the pure *Brahmam* which is none of these. The *Shabdam* will reveal the Eswaran with qualities (*Saguna*). One must feel the Eswaran with qualities. No one can explain. Where is that Eswaran with qualities? - Being the *antharaatma* of all living beings, he rules all according to *karma* and reward. The difference between the ruler as well the ruled can be seen in the *Eswaran* with qualities. The transformation does not equate to an *Eswaran* with qualities.

Hence, "God is my soul" - "I am the God within all this". This is what the *Chaanthokya Upanishat* says "*Vācārampaṉam Vikārō Nāmatēyam Mruttikā Ityēva Satyam*" – all the different nomenclature like pot etc., is only for business. The soil is the truth.

8. <u>*Atma Jnana* Tools</u> (tools for realizing the self) – Our Vedas do not say that salvation is attainable. Because what is eternal must be indistinguishable from time, space and substance. What is non-existent in one period and achievable in another is impermanent. Similarly, what does not exist in one place and is available in another is also impermanent.

The different steps or stages of knowledge of *Atman*;

Aastika Argument – There is one thing called *Atmaa* (soul). Or there is someone called God.

Aneka Jeeva Argument – There is one *Atmaa* or God in all living things

Only one *Atmaa* argument – There is only one *Atmaa* or only one God in all the living beings.

Everything lies in the *Atmaa.*

Unborn argument – There is only the *Atmaa*. Everything else is lie. Nothing else originated.

Shastras describe the devices to achieve the soul wisdom in two ways – the *Bahirangam* (open or outward) and the *Andarangam* (inner or inward).

8.1 *Bahiranga* Devices

8.1.1. *Karma Yogam* – When a *mumukshu* does not desire the rituals in which he is in whichever *Ashramam*, it gives him the cleansing power and enables him to attain the necessary qualifications for wisdom. *Karma Yoga* is not necessary to attain the fruit of wisdom. But wisdom is needed to produce.

Vedas can be divided into *Karma Kaandam* and *Jnaana Kaandam*. The Vedic parts that explain the methods of performing *karmas* are *Karma Kandam*. The *Upanishats* forming part of the *Vedanta* (the end part of the Vedas) fall into the category of *Jnana Kanda*.

Kanchi Paramaachaarya used to compare learning *Karma Kanda* to studying in schools and learning *Jnana Kanda* to studying in colleges. He used to ask – One can study in a college only after finishing the school studies. One can stop with school studies also. But is it possible to go to college without finishing school?

8.1.2. Saadana Catushtayam – In the *Brahma Sutra Bhashyam* (3.4.27), *Sri Adi Shankarar* has made it clear that the one who enjoys wisdom should be with *Nishkamya Swadharma* (self-*dharma* without any desires), the equal (*samam*), the *Damam*, etc. Wisdom, *Vairagyam*, *Samadhi-Shatka-Sampatti* and *Mumukshutvam* are the four *Sadhana Catushtayam*. According to *Brahataaranyaka Upanishat* (4.4.23) – He who knows thus, who is calm, selfless, attainable, tolerant of dualities, attains *Siddha*-peace and sees himself (*soul*).

8.2. *Andaranga* Tools

8.2.1 *Prastaana Trayam* – For the soul to be enlightened, one has to listen to the three treasures of wisdom called *Prastaana Trayam*. *Prastaanam* is the name given to the place where the God-life unity of *Tat-Tvam* is well explained. It is said that *Prastaana Trayam* (as the following list illustrates) belongs to the *Brahma Sutra*, the ten *Upanishats* and *Shrimad Bhagavad Gita*. *Sri Adi Shankara*, in his *Brahma Sutra Bhashyam* stresses that the *Mumukshu Sadhaka* should keep on doing the *Shravana-Manana-Nididhyaasana* repeatedly until the *Atma Darshan* occurs.

#	*Prastaanam*	Other Names	Texts
1.	*Shruti Prastaanam*	*Shravana Prastaanam*	Ten *Upanishats* viz., *Esha, Kena, Kata, Prashna, Mundaka, Maandukya, Taitreeya, Aitreya, Chaandokya* and *Brahadaaranyaka*
2.	*Smruti Prastaanam*	*Saadana Prastaanam*	*Shrimad Bhagavad Gita*
3.	*Darshana Prastaanam*	*Manana* or *Ukti* (Strategy) *Prastaanam*	*Brahma Sootram*

One thing to note is that in Rishikesh, Haridwar, Uttarkashi, etc., the *Prasthaanatraya Shravanam* has been continuously going on for generations. It is in this part of India that more *Sanyasis* can be found than any other parts. There, various lessons are taught with the monks as main teachers.

The three teachings for a *Sanyasi* who seek the knowledge of determination;

1. Look at everything as Eswaran
2. Save yourself through sacrifice
3. Let go of the desire/ expectation on the matters.

Note: Whatever discussed in this chapter are of some serious nature. For lay men like us, it may not be possible to comprehend the concepts through reading once. Hence it is recommended to go through more than once, to understand, comprehend and retain the perceptions.

*****

Sri Adi Shankara and the Four Mutts

Sri Adi Shankara Bhagavad Paadar, used to be affectionately addressed as *Adi Shankarar*. Typically, people would say that he was born in the year 509 B.C.E. There are some contradictions in his timeline between the Kanchi monastery and the Sringeri monastery. We are not going to get into it.

The word *Shankaracharya* consists of two parts, *Shankara* and *Acharya*. The Samskruta word *Acharya* means 'teacher'. Hence, *Shankaracharya* can also mean "one who teaches the way of *Shankara*".

Shankaracharya (शङ्कराचार्य) usually means the leader of the monasteries in the *Advaita* Vedanta tradition. This title was obtained from *Adi Shankara* himself. The priests who came in this Guru lineage are called *Shankaracharyas*.

Adi Shankara established monasteries in all the four directions of India, one for each direction. He appointed his four chief disciples as the first head of these monasteries. These are called *Aamnaaya Mutts*. These monasteries were to be run by well-informed men called *Shankaracharyas*. They will continue their priesthood of spiritual nature. The list below describes these monasteries.

#	Direction	Mutt/ *Peeta*	Disciple	*Veda*	*Maha* Sentence
1.	East	Puri Govardhana	Padmapaadar	*Rig*	*Pragnanam Brahma*
2.	South	Sringeri *Sharadha*	Sureshwarar	*Yajur*	*Aham Brahmasmi*
3.	West	*Dwarka*	Hastaamalakar	*Saama*	*Tatvamasi*
4.	North	*Jyotir Mutt*	Todakaahaaryar	*Atharva*	*Ayamaatma Brahma*

It is understood that apart from these four, one other monastery at Kanchipuram was also founded by Sri Adi Shankara and he was the first head of it.

The monastery was relocated to Kumbakonam in the middle of the 18th century to escape persecution and atrocities. Then in 1911 Mahaperiyava Paramacharyar brought back it to Kanchipuram again.

#	Mutt/ *Peeta*	Present Head(s)	Presiding Deity
1.	Puri Govardhana	Sri Nishcalaananda Saraswathi Swamy	Jagannathan
2.	Sringeri *Sharadha*	Sri Bharati Teertha Maha Swamy, Sri Vidhushekara Bharati Swamy	Sharadha
3.	*Dwarka*	Sri Swaroopaananda Saraswathi Swamy	Siddheshwar
4.	*Jyotir Mutt*	Sri Vishnu Teertha Swamy	Badri Narayanan
5.	Kanchipuram	Sri Shankara Vijayendra Saraswathi Swamy	Kamakshi

Let us read some notes and a table about each of these monasteries;

1 *Sharadha Mutt* – First *Mutt* – West –

- *Pashcinaamnaaya Mutt* – in Dwarka
- Keetawaara Sampradayam – To show kindness to all living beings right from a worm, without doing hams to all living is the Keetawaara Sampradayam.
- The yoga pattam of this mutt sanyasis are *Teertha* and *Ashrama*
- Presiding Deity – Siddheshwar
- Devi – Badra Kali
- Acharya – Vishvaroopar
- Teertham – Gomati
- Brahmachari Svaroopam

- Veda – Saama
- Maha Sentence – *Tatvamasi*
- Gotram – Avikatam
- Territories under jurisdiction – Sindhu, Souveeram, Sourashtram, Maharashtram and west India region
- In the Triveni Tirtha, those who are immersed with *Tatvamasi* are called Teerthas.
- Leaving all the desires, the ascetic with a firm mind – that is, one who is freed from the bondage of the world – is said to be Ashrama Upaadhi in the *Sannyasa* ashram.
- The one who realizes his own soul form, who adheres to *Swadharma* and who merges with his own soul bliss, is called *Swaroopar*.

2. *Govardhana Mutt* – Second *Mutt* – East –

- *Poorvaamnaaya Mutt* – in Puri
- Bhogawaara Sampradayam – Bogawaara tradition is for those who know how to avoid enjoyments etc. – that is *Bogawaara Sampradayam*.
- Forest is the dwelling place of this *ashramis*
- The yoga pattam of this mutt sanyasis are *Aaranyar*, *Teerttar* and *Ashrama*
- Kshetram – Purushottama kshetram
- Presiding Deity – Jagannathan
- Devi – Vimalaakyaa
- Acharya – Padmapaadar
- Teerttam – Mahanadi
- Brahmachari Svaroopam
- Veda – Rig
- Maha Sentence – *Pragnaanam Brahma*
- Gotram – Kashyap
- Territories under jurisdiction – Bihar, Bengal, Odisha, Magadha and East India region
- In the beautiful, uninhabited forests, the inhabitants of the forest are free from the tides. These are called '*Vanas*'
- Those who know his (Swayam) self-soul image and the strategy of the Yoga through philosophy are called '*Prakash*'.

- Those who reside in the *Aaranya* (forest) and enjoy meditating on the *Paramaatma Swaroopaa* and sacrificing whole samsara bonds are called *Aranyars*.

3. *Jyotir Mutt* – Third *Mutt* – North –

- *Uttaraamnaaya Mutt* – in Badrikashramam
- Anandawaara Sampradayam – Those who liberate animals from samsara ties are such saints as "*Anandawara*: *Sampradaayam*.
- The Principals of the House of Ananda title – Who truly understands the "Truth and Enlightenment" are meditated on and called as '*Ananda*'.
- Presiding Deity – Badri Narayanan
- Devi – Poorna Giri Devi
- Acharya – Todakaachaaryaar
- Teerttam – Alakanandaa
- Living places – Hills, mountain and other beach areas
- Veda – Atharva
- Maha Sentence – Ayamaatmaa Brahma
- Gotram – Brugvaakya
- Territories under jurisdiction – Kuru, Kashmir, Panchal and North India region
- Those who live in the mountains and forest areas, with Gita always in mind, is called '*Giri*'.
- Those who dwell on the mountaintop and realize all the essences of Brahmam as a self-conscious person will be called as '*Parvat*'.
- Those who are selected in that Brahma Sagara (ocean), who realize wisdom itself, who realize it to others and who treat others with respect will be called '*Saagar*'.

4. *Sringeri Mutt* – Fourth *Mutt* – South –

- *Dakshinaamnaaya Mutt* – in Sringeri
- Pooriwaara Sampradaayam – Puri is the name given to the one who saves his *varnashrama* and all the animals. Such a tradition is – that is *Puriwaara*: *Sampradaayam*.
- The yoga pattam of the *sanyasi*s of this mutt are Sarasvati, Bharati and Puri - *Saraswathi* is said to be the one who always speaks of

wisdom, who is poetic in speech and who holds all the essences of the world in hand. *Bharati* is said to be one who is full of knowledge, who has sacrificed everything else and who is ignorant of sorrow. Who is perfect in the philosophy of wisdom, who is perpetuated in the pure philosophy and who is known as Parabrahma, is *Puri*.

- Shetram – Rameshwar
- Presiding Deity – Adi Varaahar
- Devi – Kamakshi
- Acharya – Pritveedharar
- Veda – Yajur
- Maha Sentence – *Aham Brahmasmi*
- Gotram – Bhoorbhuva
- Territories under jurisdiction – Andhra, Dravida, Karnataka and South India region

To establish and maintain the monasteries mentioned above, *Jagadguru Adi Shankara* appointed his chief disciples as the first heads. To date, all the monasteries have been performing well.

An overview through a table

Direction	West/ Pashcinamya	East/ Poorvamnaya	North/ Uttaramnaya	South/ Dakshninamnaya	
Mutt/ Peeta	Dwarka	Puri Govardhana	Jyotir Mutt/ Badrikashrama	Sringeri	Kanchipuram
Sequence	First	Second	Third	Fourth	
Starting Year ~	491 B.C.E.	486 B.C.E.	485 B.C.E.	484 B.C.E.	482 B.C.E.
First head/ Disciple of Adi Shankara	Hastamalakar	Padmapadar	Todakachaaryar	Sureshwarar	Adi Shankarar
Yoga Titles[5]	Vana and Aaranyar	Teerttar and Ashrama	Giri, Parvata and Saagara	Saraswathi, Bharati and Puri	Indra Saraswathi
Veda	Saama	Rig	Atharva	Yajur	Rig
Sampradaya	Keetavaara:	Bhogavaara:	Aanandavaara:	Purivaara:	
Maha Sentence	Tatvamasi	Pragnaanam Brahma	Ayamaatma a Brahma	Aham Brahmaasmi	
Present Head(s)	Sri Swaroopaananda Saraswathi Swamy	Sri Nishcalaananda Saraswathi Swamy	Sri Vishnu Teertha Swamy	Sri Bharati Teertha Maha Swamy, Sri Vidhushekara Bharati Swamy	Sri Shankara Vijayendra Saraswathi Swamy
Presiding Deity	Siddheshwar	Jagannathan	Badri Narayanan	Sharadha	Kamakshi
Devi	Badra Kali	Vimalaakya a	Poorna Giri Devi	Kamakshi	Kamakshi
Teertham	Gomati	Mahanadi	Alagananda	Tungabadra	Kaveri
Svroopam	Brahmachari	Brahmachari			

[5] We can read in detail about these yoga titles in the next chapter

Heads of these five mutts, nowadays, initiate *Sanyasa*m only with their hands to their direct disciples – those who were chosen to be their successors. This was not the case earlier – many people were given asceticism. Presently, *Sanyasa*m is given to all through the heads of their Branches.

The above introduction to these five monasteries was felt necessary to understand further chapters like *Dasha Naamis*, etc. A brief note was therefore given.

*****

Sannyasa – Ten names (*Dasha Namas*)

Everyone has one or another name. Even pet animals are being called with names. In addition to individual names, most of us have a family name (sur-name) also.

Shastras have given various rules for keeping a name for babies i.e. for Naamakaranam – Brahmins to have the surname or suffix as 'Sharma', Kshatrias to have 'Varma', Vysyas to have 'Gupta' and others as 'Dasa'. In some places the village name itself is had as surname. In addition, people may choose to have various surnames.

*Sanyasa*m is treated as a new birth[6] – being born in a new family – as Guru race. Guru used to keep a *Sannyasa* name. In addition, he would also keep the disciple a family name. Those who follow the ascetic order in Hinduism, according to their tradition, take one of these ten (*Sannyasa*) surnames.

1. Saraswathi
2. Teerttar
3. Aranyar
4. Bharati
5. Ashrama
6. Giri
7. Parvata
8. Saagara
9. Vana
10. Puri – Since originated in the Swami Thotha Puri Guru race, the Swamis of the Ramakrishna Mission will join the Puri lineage.

[6] When we talk about the janma star of a sanyasi, it should not be the star of his birth in this world. It should be star of the day on which he took Sanyasam. His name has changed and hence his birth star also. Is it not the Sanyasam a new birth? Further in particular, his poorvashrama birth is to be treated as ended. Still when considered in depth, the thithi of the sanyasa day has to be considered and not even the star. It is conventional that Adi Shankara jayanthi is celebrated on Shukla Panchami and not with any star.

We earlier studies that Sri Sankara had four *Sanyas*i disciples, viz., Suresvara, Padmapada, Hastamalaka and Totaka. Suresvara was in charge of Sringeri Mutt, Padmapada was in charge of Puri Mutt, Hastamalaka was in charge of Dvaraka Mutt and Totaka was in charge of Joshi-Mutt.

- The *Sanyasi*s of Sringeri Mutt, the spiritual descendants of Sri Sankara and Suresvaracharya, have three titles, viz., Sarasvati, Puri and Bharati.
- The *Sanyasi*s of the Dvaraka Mutt have two titles, viz., Teertha and Ashrama.
- The *Sanyasi*s of the Puri Mutt have two titles, viz., Vana and Aranya.
- The *Sanyasi*s of the Joshi-Mutt have three titles, viz., Giri, Parvata and Sagara.

Some more vital points to note;

- The Dashanamis worship Lord Siva or Lord Vishnu and meditate on Nirguna Brahmam.
- The Dandi *Sanyasi*s, who hold staff in their hands, belong to the order of Sri Shankara.
- Paramahamsa *Sanyasi*s do not hold staff. They freely move about as itinerant monks.
- The Avadhoota *Sannyasa* Ashram fits in all above the ten types. That is its greatness. They are supposed to be naked *Sanyas*is. They should not keep any property with them.
- The saints of the Kanchi monastery, the spiritual descendants of Sri Adi Shankara, hold the yoga title of *Ananda Saraswathi*. However, this yoga title does not form part of Dasha Naama. This can be considered as sub-set Saraswathi Yoga title.
- The *sanyasi*s of the Ramakrishna Mission are also part of the Sri Adi Shankara Order. They have the title of Puri. Yet they do not keep the *dandam* in their hands.

The name Saraswathi is related to '*Vak*'. Hence, the names Saraswathi, Teertha and Bharti are becoming more and more learned.

Those who have the name Puri worship Saguna Brahmam and they have various ritual to practice.

The above ten named persons have a different attitude in their practice, but with regard to the moksha device – the goal of achieving Brahmam all are one the same. In this angle they do not differ.

All of these names are considered "*yoga pattam*" (yoga title). The Swamiji's should be asked as "What is your yoga pattam?" and not as "What *Sannyasa* family do you belong to?" Also, they should not be asked as "What is your name?".

There were no such names before the time of Adi Shankara. The names were like Goudapada, Bhagavad Pada, Govinda Bhagavad Pada, Adi Shankara Bhagavat Pada and so on.

Dasha naami Sampradayam or Tradition refers to the Yogic title of the *Sanyas*is, who were descended from Adi Shankara tradition, holding one Dandam in a hand, to observe the Hindu Religion. They are followers of Advaita Vedanta. They are also called Dasha naami genealogies. Each monastery and yoga titles were also described above.

Adi Shankara founded the monasteries to spread his doctrines and advaita philosophies in Sringeri and other centers. Devout devotees made substantial donations to these monasteries. Over time number of these monasteries increased. Many other assets came under the control of these monks. That way the ten Advaita *Sannyasa* names arose as above.

The disciples of Ra*manu*ja and Madhvar also have many monasteries of their own. Vallabhacharya (one of the great Acharyas who explained the Vedanta Shastras) and his disciples did not accept the *Sannyasa* order. According to them in the age of Kali, asceticism, along with its rules, should be sacrificed. They acted as devotees, like Uttawa (Shrimad Bhagavatam III.4), except they did not observe the fourth Ashram.

*****

Rules to Adopt *Sanyasam*

It is somewhat doubtful whether the *Chaandogya Upanishat* regarded *Sannyasa* as the fourth and the last stage in a man's life when ideally planned. It merely states that— 'one that holds fast by the realization of brahmam attains immortality'. But it appears that a stage of the abandonment of worldly riches, a life of begging and contemplation of the Absolute and its realization had been known to the earliest *Upaniṣats* like the *Bruhaadaaranyaka*. Whether it was the fourth stage or whether it could be reached even in the stage of *brahmacarya* or of a house-holder (grihastha) is left in doubt so far as the older *Upaniṣats* are concerned. The *Jaabaalopaniṣat* has been quoted to show that it gave an option either to regard *sannyasa* as the 4th stage in a man's life or to resort to it immediately after any of the first two *āśramas*.

After leaving home, wife, children and possessions, be should dwell outside the villages, should be homeless and stay under a tree or in an un-inhabited house wherever he may be when the sun sets and should always wander from place to place; but he may remain in one place only in the rainy season. Śaṅkha allows him to stay in one place only for two months in the rains, while Kanva says that be may stay one night in a village and five in a town (except in the rains). When he follows the rule of staying four or two months in one place, he should do so from the full moon of *Āṣāḍha* or an ascetic may always stay on the banks of the Ganges.

Before looking at the practices of taking *sannyasa*, let us see who is eligible to take *sannyasa*.

One important question on which opinion was sharply divided is whether *sannyasa* was allowed to all the three *varṇas* or only to *Brahmins*. Let us refer some *shastra* evidences in this regard;

'This Self brahmins seek to know by the study of the *Veda*'; *Brahadaaranyaka Upanishat* IV.4.22 states — After knowing this Self, brahmins give up the hankering after progeny, wealth and heavenly worlds and practice begging.

Brahadaaranyaka Upanishat (III.5.1) continues – Closely examining the worlds that are the rewards of actions, a brahmin should come to be disgusted etc.

Mundaka Upanishat (I.2.12) – Closely examining the worlds that are the rewards of actions, a brahmin should come to be disgusted etc.

Here, the word *'brahmin'* being used, śruti indicates that brahmins alone can be *sanyasi*s.

Manu (VI. 38) begins his description of the 4th stage with the words — 'a brahmin should leave his house and go into the world as a wanderer' and winds up the chapter (VI.97) by saying — 'I have declared this fourfold procedure in relation to brahmins'.

The Jabālopaniṣat ordains — 'whether a man has fulfilled his *vratas-samavartanas*[7] or not, whether he has performed *samāvartana* (the ceremonial bath after studying Veda) or not, whether his fires (Vedic) have ceased or not he should resort to the wandering ascetic's life the very day on which he feels disgust with mundane affairs'.

It thus allows even a brahmacārī to become an ascetic; a kshatriya and vaiśya could be a brahmacarī. Yājnavalkeeyam (III.32) states that *Sannyasa* is a means of purification (of the mind) in the case of twice-born classes. Besides the only condition precedent mentioned by the *Jabālopaniṣat* for resorting to *pravrāja* (ascetic life) is *vairagya* and whoever feels the latter is authorized to betake himself to that stage. Yājnavalkeeyam (III.61) while laying down the observances of ascetics employs the word *'dvijaḥ'* and not *'brāhmanaḥ'*.

Both these opposing views are supported by the most famous authors. The first view that only brahmins can be *Sanyasi*s is affirmed by the great *Śaṅkarācārya* in his *Bhashyam* for *Brahadaranyaka Upanishat* III.5.1 and IV.5.15. It is most interesting and also very

[7] *Guru* performs *Upanayanam* to the student and takes him to *Gurukulam* for studies of *Vedas*. After teaching all the 4 *Vedas* he performs 4 *Vratas* (graduation ceremonies) for the disciple. *Samaavartanam* is a part of it.

refreshing that *Sureshvara* in his *Vārtika* on *Śaṅkara's Bhashyam* on *Brahadaranyaka Upanishat* III.5.1 first explains the views of his *guru*, then enters the lists against his great master and combats his views with cogent arguments. Most of the medieval writers and works such as *Medhātithi* on *Manu* (VI.97), the *Smruti-mukta-phala* uphold the view that only brahmins can resort to the 4th *āśrama*, while a few works like the *Smruti-Chandrika* support the second view.

So far as the *smriti* texts and the medieval works are concerned a śūdra could not become a *sanyasi*. The *Shanti-parva* (63. 11-14) is quite dear that a *śūdra* cannot be a *bhikṣu*. It also (18. 32) informs us that in its day many (probably including śūdras) assumed the outward signs of the 4th *āśrama*, got their heads tonsured and moved about in ochre-coloured garments (*kāśāya*) for securing alms and gifts. But there are clear indications that *śūdras* did assume even in the times of ancient smṛtis the ascetic's garb and mode of life. When the *Āśrama-vāsika-parva* 26.33 states that *Vidura* was buried as an ascetic, the commentator *Nīlakaṇṭha* remarks that this indicates that even *śūdras* can follow the mode of the ascetic life.

It appears that even women could in rare cases adopt the ascetic's life in ancient Brahminic times. The *Maitreyar* on *Yājnavalkeeyam* III.58 quotes a *sūtra* of *Boudayanam* (*strinām caike*) to the effect that according to some *ācāryas* even women could adopt the ascetic mode of life. *Patañjali* in his *Mahābhāṣya* speaks of a woman ascetic (*parivrājaka*) named *Śaṅkarā*.

In the drama called *Mālavikāgnimitra*, *Kalidāsa* describes the *Paṇḍitā Kausikī* as wearing the garb of an ascetic (I.14). It must be said that the general trend of Hinduism is against women adopting the homeless or ascetic life. The *Jātakas* (IV. 392) rarely speak of *caṇḍālas* as adopting the homeless condition

Enough of qualifications. Let us discuss the process of adopting *Sannyasa*;

Jabālopaniṣat says – In the process of adopting *Sannyasa*, a person has to first do sacrifice to *Prajapati*. Whatever assets he had should be donated to Brahmins, poor and orphans. Sacrifice should be done through holy fire also.

The *Narasimha Purana* 58.36 allows everyone who is a *Vedic* student to become an ascetic if his tongue, his sexual emotions, his appetite for food and his speech are pure (i.e. under strict control). Further he is allowed to become a *Sanyasi* only if his speech is pure.

The *Narasimha Purana* (60.2-4) requires that before entering upon this order one should perform eight *srāddhas*. They are;

1. *Daiva* (to *Vasus, Rudras, Ādityas*),
2. *Ārṣa* (to the ten sages viz. *Marīci* and others),
3. *Divya* (to *Hiraṇyagarbha* and *Vairāja*),
4. *Manuṣya* (to *Sanaka, Sanandana* and five others),
5. *Bhoutika* (to five elements, *pṛthvī*, etc.),
6. *Paitṛka* (to *Kavyavad* fire, Soma, Aryaman, Pitṛs called Agniśvatta etc.)
7. *Matṛsrāddha* (to ten mothers such as Gaurī, Padma et al),
8. *Ātma-śrāddha* (self or to Paramātman).

Manu is careful to point out (VI. 35-37) that a man should fix his mind on *moksha* after studying the Veda, procreating sons, performing sacrifices i.e. after discharging his debts to the sages, the pitṛs and gods.

Boudhayana Dharma Sutra II.10.3-6 states that a householder who has no children or whose wife is dead or who has established his children in the path of *dharma* or who is over 70 years of age may become an ascetic.

The description of the *Boudhayana Dharma Sutra* being probably the most ancient among extant works is briefly set out below —

After having cut the hair on the head, the beard, the hair on the body, the nails, he makes ready three sticks (three *Dandams*), a loop of strings, (a piece of cloth as) a water strainer, a jar and a bowl. Having taken these, he should go to the end of his village, or to the extremity of the boundary of his village, or the fire-hall; he should partake of ghee, milk and curds (mixed together) and should fast or drink water. Then he should recite the *vyāhrtis* separately preceded by *'Om'* and followed by the words — 'I enter the *Savitrī*' and by one *pāda* of the sacred *Gāyatrī* and then all together[8].

Before sunset, he heaps fuel on the gārhapatya fire (if he has maintained Vedic fires), brings the *anvahāryapacana* (*dakṣināgni*) to the spot, takes the flaming *āhavanīya* fire out of the gārhapatya, melts ghee on the *gārhapatya*, cleanses it (with blades of *kuśa*, the *darba* grass), takes four portions of the butter in the spoon called *'sruk'* and offers in the *āhavanīya* fire on which fuel-sticks have been heaped a full oblation (i.e. whole spoonful) four times saying *'Om svāha'*. This is called *Brahmanvadhāna* (putting fuel-sticks on fire for securing knowledge of brahmam).

Then in the evening after *agnihoṭra* has been offered, he strews grass to the north of the *gārhapatya* fire, places on the grass sacrificial vessels in pairs with the upper parts turned downwards, spreads *darbha* grass to the south of the *āhavanīya* fire on the seat meant for the brahma priest, covers it with black antelope skin and remains awake the whole of that night.

Then he rises at the time (*muhurta*) sacred to Brahma (very early morning) and offers *agnihoṭra* in the morning at the proper time. Then after covering the part of the altar called *pṛṣṭyā* and bringing water he prepares an offering for *Agni Vaiśvanara* cooked on twelve potsherds. That well-known *iṣṭi* will be the last he will perform. Afterwards, he throws in the *āhavanīya* fire those sacrificial vessels which are not made of stone or earth. And throwing the two *araṇis* (the sticks by the friction of which fire was produced for Vedic rites) into the *gārhapatya* fire with the words— 'may you two be of one mind with us', he (mentally) deposits the three fires in himself. Repeating the *mantra* – *'yā te agne yajñiya tanur'* (*Taitreeya* III.4. & 10.5) he inhales the smell of the smoke of each of the three fires thrice. Then standing within the sacrificial enclosure he says thrice in a low voice and thrice aloud the words *"om bhūḥ, bhuvaḥ svaḥ"*. I have entered the order of *Sannyasa* (I have

---

[8] The central ideas of the ceremony are the renunciation of all worldly ties, contempt of the world and all earthly riches, a life of *ahiṃsā* and contemplation on and realization of the Absolute *Brahmam*.

abandoned my worldly desires), I have entered the order of *Sannyasa*, I have entered the order of *Sannyasa*'. Lastly, he pours out as much water as will fill his joined hands saying — "I promise that no injury will proceed from me to any creature". He must henceforward restrain his speech. He holds his staff saying — 'thou art my friend, protect me'. He takes the *śika* (loop of strings) with the words — *"yadasya pare rajasaḥ"* (*Taitreeya* IV.2.5.2); he takes the cloth for straining water with the text — *"yena devaḥ pavitrena"* (*Taitreeya Brahmana* 1.4.8 and *Nirukta* V.6); he takes the water jar reciting — *"yena deva jyotiṣordhvam"* (Taitreeya V.7.2.2); he takes the bowl after reciting the seven *vyāhrtis*. Taking with him the staffs, the loop of strings, the cloth as a water strainer, the water-pot and the bowl he goes to a place where water can be had, bathes, sips water and sprinkles himself (performs *mārjana*) with the *Surabhimatī* verse (*dadhi-krāvno*, Rig IV.39.6), with *Ablingā* verses, *Varuṇī* verses, *Hiraṇyavarṇā* verses (*Taitreeya* 6.1.1 & *Atharva Veda* I.33. 1-4) and *Pavamanī* verses (Rig IX.1 etc.). While still in the water he performs sixteen *prāṇāyāmas* after (mentally going over) the *Agahamarṣana* verses (Rig X.190.1-3), comes out of the water on the bank, wrings his garments, puts on another pure (washed) garment, sips water, takes the cloth for straining water with the words — *'om bhuḥ bhuvaḥ svaḥ'* and performs *tarpaṇa* with seven *vyāhrtis*. He then fills his joined hands with water and performs *tarpaṇa* to the *Manes* just in the same way as he did to the gods, then he worships the Sun with the two verses *udu tyam* (Rig 1.50.1) and *citram* (Rig 115.1). He then offers *tarpaṇa* to the *Atman* (self) with —

- The syllable *Oṃ* is *brahmam*;
- This light (the Sun) that diffuses warmth is indeed *brahmam*;
- This which gives warmth is indeed the *Veda*;
- This indeed that sheds warmth is the (proper) object of knowledge';

Then he worships the *Atman* with the words— 'the Self is *Brahmam*, it is light'. Let him repeat the *Gayatri mantra* an unlimited number of times or at least one thousand times. Repeating — *'om bhurbhuvaḥ svaḥ'*, he takes up the water strainer (cloth) and fetches water.

Let him not thereafter perform *ācamana* with water that has not been drawn up (from a well), which has not been strained and which has not been completely cleansed. Let him not wear thereafter white garments. He may carry one staff or three.

He has to keep the following vows —

- Ahiṃsā (abstaining from injury to any creature),
- Truthfulness,
- Not depriving others of any property of theirs,
- Continence and
- Liberality.

There are five minor *vratas* (vows) viz.

- Absence of anger,
- Waiting upon the guru,
- Avoidance of carelessness (or rashness),
- Cleanliness,
- Purity in food.

Then follow rules as to begging for alms. When he returns from begging, he places the alms in a pure spot, washes his hands and feet and announces (the alms) first to the Sun with the verses — *'udu tyam* (Rig 1.50.1) and *'citram'* (Rig I.115.1); he also announces the alms to *Brahmam* with the text — *'brahma jajñanam'* (Taitreeya Samhita IV.2.8.2 & *Atharva Veda* IV.1.1).

It is declared (in Vedic texts) that after the *brahmādhāna* the sacred fires are contained in the sacrificer himself; his *prāṇa, apāna, vyāna, udāna* and *samāna* represent the five fires *gārhapatya, anvahāryapacana* (*dakṣinagni*), *āhavanīya, sabhya* and *avasathya*. These five fires indeed abide in the *Atman*; he, therefore, offers (the oblations) to the *Atman* only. This sacrifice offered in the soul, which is centered in and based on the *Atman*, leads the soul to bliss. Giving compassionately portions of the alms to creatures and sprinkling the remainder with water, he should partake of it as if it were some medicine. After he has taken the food and taken *ācamana* he worships the Sun with the *Jyotismatī* verse viz. *"ud vayam"* (Rig I.50.10) after inaudibly muttering the two texts— *"vāṅ me āsan"* (Taitreeya Samhita

V.5.9.2) and *"nasoḥ prāṇāḥ"* (*Taitreeya Aranyaka* X.72). Let him eat food given without asking, regarding which nothing has been settled beforehand and which comes to him by chance and so much only as is necessary to support life.

Now they quote the following rules for the case where the teachers explain the *Upaniṣat* — 'standing (in the day), keeping silence, sitting (at night) in the posture of crossed legs, bathing thrice a day, he shall subsist entirely on rice grains, oil-cake, food from barley, sour milk and milk'.

It is declared in Vedic texts — on that occasion he shall keep strict silence and converse as much as is necessary with the teachers deeply versed in the three *Vedas*, with ascetics or other learned persons in the several *āśramas*, after pressing the teeth together, all the while contemplating on what he hears, but not in such a way as would cause a breach of his vow. He may keep only one of the rules out of the three viz. standing (in the day), rigid silence and sitting with crossed legs (at night) and not altogether. Eight things do not cause him who is intent on vows as above to break his own vow viz. water, roots, ghee, milk, sacrificial food, the wish of a brahmin, an order of his *guru* and medicine.

Let him mutter the *mantras* in the evening and morning that are repeated in the *Agnihoṭra*. He should perform his evening *Sandhya* adoration with *mantras* addressed to *Varuṇa* and in the morning with those addressed to *Mitra* (Rig III.59). It is declared in the *Veda*— "limited in number are the *Rig* verses, the *sāmans* and the *yajus* verses, but there is no limit to this that is *brahmam*". In this way (i.e. repeating *om*) the ascetic may give up the rest of the *Vedas*, but should stand firm by the root of the *Vedas* (viz. *om*). The Veda is the tree and its root is *prāṇava* (*om*). He should meditate on *'om'*. *Prajapati* has declared that *prāṇava* leads on to union with *Brahmam*. Let him cleanse the vessel of brahmam with seven *vyāhrtis*.

Among medieval works the *Smrtyārthasāra*, the *Smruti*, the *Yati-dharma*, the *Nirnaya-sindhu* (III) and the *Dharma-sindhu* give various detailed procedures. The procedure in the *Dharma-sindhu* contains the following major elements —

- *Sannyasa* has to be resorted to in the northward passage of the Sun (Uttarayana – From Mid-January to Mid-July). For a man who is about to die, even in the southward passage (*Dakshinayana*) is ok.
- He should find out a teacher possessed of the virtues of quiescence and note for three months the duties of ascetics in his company, should purify himself with *japa* of the sacred *Gayatri, Rudra mantras* and by *Kooṣmāṇḍa homa* (Taitreeya Aranyaka II.7).
- He should then make a resolute (sankalpa) after reciting the place and time on a proper tithi and should perform the *prāyaścitta* of *catuḥ-kṛshra* by giving a cow or money.
- Then he should begin to perform on the 11th or 12th day, 16 *śrāddhas* for himself and *sapindīkaraṇa*. Then he is to perform eight *śrāddhas* (as already mentioned) and *tarpaṇa* as a subordinate part (*anga*) of these eight *śrāddhas*.
- On the day these eight *śrāddhas* are performed or on the next day he should shave off the whole head after keeping about six hairs out of his top-knot, pare his nails and then take his bath.
- Then he is to donate to brahmins and his sons all his wealth except his wearing apparel and the materials for *homa*.
- The garments he is to wear should be dyed with red chalk; he should secure a bamboo staff as high as his head etc., and as thick as his thumb finger and brought by a brahmin; that staff should be sprinkled over with water from a conch to the accompaniment of '*om*', the *puruṣa* hymn (Rig X:90) and such names (of *Viṣṇu*) as *Kesava*, etc.
- He should also keep ready a water jar, a strip for his loins and a garment to cover his body and a blanket and *pādukas* (sandals).
- He should declare his resolve (*sankalpa*) to become a *Sanyasi* and perform the worship of *Ganesa, punyāha-vācana*, worship of mother goddesses and *Nāndī-śrāddha*. He should then perform *japa* by saying '*namaḥ*' to *Brahma* (in the dative), *Viṣṇu, Rudra, Surya, Soma, Ātman, Antarātman, Paramātman* and also repeat the first *padas* of each of the four *Vedas*.
- He should then eat three handfuls of barley flour with '*om*' and touch his navel. He should then sip thrice ghee or water mixed with milk and curds repeating the mantras *trivṛd-asi, pravṛd-asi* and *vivṛd-asi* and then drink water with the *mantra* – 'may the waters

purify' (*Taitreeya* Aranyaka 10.23), then perform *ācamana* and declare his resolve to fast.

- Then comes *Savitrī-praveśa*; then he should kindle his *gṛhya* fire or if he has no *gṛhya* fire then he should bring domestic fire with the *mantra* – *"pṛṣṭo divi"* (Rig VII.5.27) and kindle it with the three mantras '*tat savituḥ*', '*tāṃ savituḥ*' and '*viśvāni deva*' (Rig III. 62.10, Vaj. S-17.74, Rig V.82.5).
- Then comes *brahmānvādhāna* before sunset. He should thereafter perform evening *Sandhya* adoration, *homa* and *vaiśvadeva* and keep awake the whole night near the fire.

Then the next morning after the daily *homa* and *Vaiśvadeva* he should offer a mess of cooked food to *Agni* or *Vaiśvanara* and perform the homa to *prāna* and others, the *puruṣa sūkta* homa and *Virāja* homa. The *Virāja* homa is a lengthy performance and the principal elements in it are — the offering of 40 oblations of each out of the three viz. fuel-sticks, boiled rice and ghee after repeating certain verses such as — "may my five *prāṇas* be purified, may I be light (illumination) free from *rajas* (the principle of activity or obstruction) and from evil, *svāhā*; this is for the prāṇa and the rest, it is not mine".

In this way oblations are offered to five senses, the mind, buddhi, seed, thought and *sankalpa*, to the constituents of the body, to the several limbs of the body (head, hands and feet etc..), to *purusa* and others, to the five elements, to the five *guṇas* of the elements, to the five *kośas* (sheaths) and several others. Then an oblation of *ājya* (ghee) is made to *Prajapati*. Then he should recite the *Purusa* hymn (Rig X.90) and the first sentences of the four *Vedas*, offer oblations to *Agni Sviṣṭakṛt*, distribute gifts to students and others, he should burn his wooden utensils in his *gṛhya* fire if he has kept one and donate the metal vessels to his *guru*, then he should deposit the fire in himself by reciting *"ayam te yoniḥ"* (Rig III. 29.10) and *"ya te agne yajñiya"* (Taitreeya Samhita III.4.10.5) thrice and should face and take in the blaze and warmth of his *gṛhya* fire, should take a black antelope skin and leave his house.

He should give blessings to his sons and other near relatives and bid good-bye to them with the words— "to me belongs no one nor do I belong to any one".

Then he should go to a reservoir of water, take in his folded hands water and offer it to all gods with the hymn Rig X.103 (1-13). He should declare a resolve to resort to *Sannyasa* for the realization of *brahmam* and offer three handfuls of water in the reservoir. He should then discharge water into the reservoir from his joined hands saying— "I have given up the hankering for sons, wealth, worlds and for everything) may there be safety to all creatures from me, *svāhā*".

Then he should again declare that he has abandoned everything, all pleasures, all sentiments of anger etc., all joys of flowers, scents, dancing and music, all duties of *varna* and *āśramas* etc.; he should also declare— "I shall not cause any injury to any creature in thought, word or by the body; may all creatures have no fear of me".

He should think of the Sun and other gods as witnesses to this declaration and standing in navel-deep water should again perform the *Savitrī-praveśa* and offer water in declaring— "I have risen beyond the desire for sons, worlds and wealth and shall practice begging".

After this comes the utterance of the *praiśa* (the call or direction). In a low, moderate and loud voice the entrant should declare— *"om, bhooḥ* – I have given up everything! *Oṃ bhuvaḥ*, I have given up everything!, *Oṃ svah*, I have given up everything!, *Oṃ bhur bhuvaḥ svah*, I have given up everything" and should discharge water in the reservoir of water with the words— "may there be no injury to all creatures from me, *svāhā*".

He should pluck out the topknot, take out his sacred thread[9] and hold them in his hand and offer them in water with water with the words — 'water is indeed all deities, I sacrifice (the top-knot and sacred thread) to all gods, *svāhā*' and then he should send up a prayer to *Vasudeva*.

Then he should remove his wearing apparel and walk five steps with his face to the north.

---

[9] One Swamijee, during discussions with the author of this book, in the lighter way said, "my father spent ₹500 and gave me sacred thread at my 5th age and at the 18th age I spent ₹50,000 to remove it".

Then the *ācārya* should bow to the entrant and should hand over to the latter a piece of loin cloth and upper garment and a staff. The entrant should wear them and hold the staff with appropriate *mantras* and also a water jar and an *āsana* (a seat).

He should then hold a fuel-stick in his hand, bow to his *guru*, sit down in the eagle posture and make a request to the *guru* in the words— "Oh teacher, who are like the Lord of the Universe to me, save me who am scorched by the fire of *samsara* and who am bitten by Death; I have thrown myself on your mercy" and also repeat the verse— *"yo brahman"* (*Svetasvatara Upanishat* VI. 18). Having waited upon the *guru* with these words and placing his right knee on the ground, he should clasp the feet of his guru and should say— "teach, Sir, Brahmam to me".

The *guru* should contemplate on his Self as *Brahmam*, should recite over a conch full of water the sacred syllable *'om'* twelve times, should pour the water from the conch on his disciple, should recite the propitiatory verse — *'shannomitraḥ'* (Rig I.90.9), then lay his hand on the head of the disciple, should recite the *Puruṣa* hymn (Rig X.90), should place his hand on the heart of the disciple and mutter the *mantra* – "I place thy heart in disciplined obedience to me",[10] the *guru* should then mutter in the right ear of the disciple the syllable *'om'* and should enlighten him about the significance of *'om'* and of *pañci-karaṇa*; he should then impart to the disciple one of the four great *Veda* sentences (*mahāvakya*) *"prajñānam brahma"* (*Aitreya Upanishat* III.3), *"ayam-ātma brahma"* (*Brahadaaranyaka Upanishat* II.5.19), *"tat tvam-asi"* (Chandogya Upanishat VI.8.7) and *"aham brahmāsmi"* (*Brahadaaranyaka Upanishat* I.4.10) in accordance with the tradition of his school and enlighten him about the meaning thereof.

---

[10] *Mama vrate hṛdyam te dadāmi* ... This occurs in in *upaṇayana* where the teacher addresses the boy in these words. The same words are addressed in the marriage rites by the bridegroom to the bride (where *prajāpati* substituted for *brihaspati*).

Then he should give to the disciple a *deeksha* name and a yoga pattam like *tīrtha*, *āśrama*, etc., according to the tradition of his order.

Then the *guru* may bring about what is called *paryanka-śauca* (purification by being seated on a stool etc.) may be briefly described.

On an auspicious day a householder seats the ascetic in front of him on a wooden stool or seat, places five heaps of earth to his left and also to his right and also pure water on both sides. Then the householder simultaneously washes the two knees of the ascetic with water and earth from the first heap of earth on the left. Then he should wash his own left hand with earth and water taken from the half of the first heap on the right and with the remaining half of the first heap on the right he should wash both his hands seven times with the same water. With the second heap on the left he should wash simultaneously the two thighs (janghā) of the ascetic four times and with one half of the second heap on the right he should wash his own left hand seven times and with the other half of the second heap (on the light) he should wash both his hands four times. The ankle, the upper part of the foot and the lower park (sole) of the foot of the ascetic are respectively washed with the third, fourth and fifth heap on the left and his own left hand and both hands are washed a certain varying number of times with 3rd, 4th, 5th heaps on the right.

After the ascetic has undergone paryanka-śauca, he should cleanse his waist, wear a string round his waist and his loin cloth and cover his waist with a piece of cloth. He should then sit with his guru's permission on a high seat and should propound some *Vedānta* topic in the presence of the persons assembled. The ascetic guru should sprinkle on the head of his ascetic disciple water from a conch to the accompaniment of the *Purusha* hymn (Rig X 90), should honour him by offering clothes, sandalwood paste, flowers, incense, lamp and naivedya. He (the *guru*) should hold a piece of cloth over the head of the disciple, recite along with the other yatis the chapter called *Viśvarūpa* (11th chapter of the *Bhagavad-gīta*) from the 15th verse to the 33rd verse. He should then give the name already determined upon to the disciple and say to him— "Henceforward you may admit to sannyasa one who is eligible for it, initiate him and give him the yoga-paṭṭa". Then the disciple bows to the yatis older than himself. Then the guru gives to the disciple a waist-thread and a staff marked with five *mudras* and should offer his own salutation to the disciple according to the tradition of his order. Other ascetics and house-holders also should bow to the disciple, who should only repeat the word *'Narāyaṇa'*, should leave the high seat and seat his guru thereon, should bow to the guru according to the rules of the order and to the other ascetics.

Thus, he has fully entered into *Sanyasam* and start to live the life of an ascetic.

Shastras insist on the sequence of *Brahmacaryam, Grahastam, Vaana Prastam* and then to enter *Sanyasam*. However, depending on the maturity of the mind, a person can take up *Sanyasam* from *Grahastaashramam* or even from *Brahmacaryam*. Best example for the same is *Sri Adi Shankarar*. More people taking *sanyasam* from *Brahmacaryam* has come into practice only after *Sri Adi Shankarar*.

Still, people taking *sanyasam* from *Grahastam* is also in vogue. *Aapastamba* himself, has not much stressed *Vaana Prastam* during the era of *Kali*. Hence taking *sanyasam* from *Grahastam* is also an acceptable one only.

When people take *sanyasam* from *Brahmacaryam*, mother has to give permission. *Sri Adi Shankarar* did a drama that his leg has been caught by a crocodile and all, just to get permission from his mother. All of us are aware of this drama.

Similarly, people taking *sanyasam* from *Grahastashramam* has to get permission from wife. This is very important.

When mother or wife, as the case may be giving permission, it is customary that the person taking Sannyasa used to give a boon to her. Again, coming to the story of *Adi Shankarar* he gave a boon to his mother, that he would come back to her, during her last hours and even do her last rites, thought that have been prohibited by the *shastras*.

We are aware of many people whose minds have matured in order to attain *Brahmam* without taking up any such asceticism. The main example is *Shuka Brahmam*, a son of *Veda Vyasa*. Although he lived with his wife for a very short time and had children, he soon became known as *Shukabrahmam* after meditating on the nature of *Brahmam*. He knew the nature of Brahma even before marriage. For some time in his married life, he was reluctant to accept his father's compulsion (King Janaka also insisted to listen to his father's word and get married).

Ramakrishna Paramahamsar, who lived in the 19th century, was not formally enlightened into *Sannyasa*. Alongwith his wife Sharda Devi, however and he lived as a couple, yet as monks. He also received the title *Paramahamsa*.

His disciple, Swami Vivekananda, went one step ahead, lived as a *Naishtika Brahmacari*[11], delved into Vedanta and realized *Brahmam*. He received the title of Swami and lived with light red dress.

Ramana Maharishi, who lived in the last century, realized the Brahmam even as a boy and is known as 'Bhagavan' by all.

Krupaananda Warrior, who lived in the last century, was not a formal ascetic. Yet as a couple with his wife, he lived like a monk. His life itself ended in the sky (while flying in a plane).

What we learn from these all, is that maturity of mind and realizing Atman/ Brahmam is the only key parameter. All these ascetic practices, procedures, rules, etc., are all devices/ tools. It is very good if one can attain Brahmam without all these also. That is also acceptable.

*****

[11] The concept of *Chaitanyar* has been discussed in another chapter in detail.

Obligations of a *Sanyasi*

Many Rishis, many shastras, say different things about the duties of a *sanyasi*. Generally, once he has attained asceticism, one has to leave home and live outside the villages after sacrificing one's wife, children and all possessions. He has to be homeless. Must live under a tree or in a dilapidated house where no one lives. He must always wander from place to place. He can stay wherever he is at sunset; He has been permitted to stay continuously in one place during the Rainy Season, for 2 months.

Sage Kanva says – Staying in a village for more than one day, in a city for more than 5 days (in different corners of the city) outside of the rainy season is called 'residence'. During rainy season, when he decides to stay in the same place for 2 or 4 months, then he has to start from *Ashada* (June – July) full moon day or he can stay in the banks of river Ganges.

Dakṣa Prajapati (VII. 34-38) emphasizes this point very well — He should always wander alone without a companion, as by so doing he will be free from attachments and the pangs of separation. The real ascetic always stays alone; if two stay together, they form a pair; if three stay together they are like a village and if more (than three stay together) then it becomes like a town. An ascetic should not form a pair or a village or a town; by so doing he swerves from his dharma, since (if two or more stay together) they begin to exchange news about the ruling prince, about the alms obtained and by close contact sentiments of affection, jealousy or wickedness arise between them. Bad ascetics engage in many activities viz. expounding (texts) for securing money or honour and also gathering pupils round them. There are only four proper actions for an ascetic and no fifth viz. contemplation, purity, begging, always staying alone.

Gathering disciples not out of compassion but for service, profit and honour constitutes "gathering of disciples". Any conversation other than on spiritual topics discourses on Dharma, requesting alms, prayer, offering words of kindness or condolence or asking directions is called "idle conversation".

And to collect students. There are only four right actions for a monk - thought, purity, pixie and always being alone, nothing fifth.

Nārada says — there are six acts which ascetics must do as if ordered by the king under the threat of a penalty viz. begging, japa, contemplation, bath (thrice daily), purity and worship of Siva or Viṣṇu. He should be celibate, should always be devoted to contemplation and spiritual knowledge and should be unattached to all objects of sense and pleasure.

He should move about avoiding all trouble or injury to creatures, should make all creatures safe with him, should bear with indifference all disrespect, should entertain no anger towards him who is furious with him, should utter benedictions over him also who runs him down, should never utter an untruth.

Some special rules are laid down about the *ahnika* (daily rites) of ascetics. They have to perform *śauca*, brushing the teeth, bath, just as house-holders have to do. *Manu* (V.137), *Viṣṇu Dharma Sutram* (60. 26, *Śaṅkha* 16.23-24) says that forest hermits and ascetics have respectively to perform three and four times as much *śauca* (bodily purification) as house-holders.

Certain rules are laid down for an ascetic as regards giving and receiving honour or salutation. An ascetic should bow to gods and to older ascetics who act according to the rules of their order, but should not offer *namaskāra* to a house-holder even if the latter be well-conducted. If another person bows to an ascetic, the latter should not pronounce any benediction but should only utter the word 'Nārāyaṇa'.

When an ascetic (even one who has taken *Sannyasa* on his death-bed) dies, he is to be buried and not cremated. No mourning is to be observed for a *yati* when he dies (Atri 97) and no śrāddhas are to be offered on his death except the pārvana on the 11th day after death (vide Aparārka).

If an ascetic hears of the death of his purvashrama son or any other purvashrama relative, he does not become impure and has not to bathe but on hearing of his puorvashrama mother's or purvashrama father's death he has to bathe, though he observes no mourning.

According to the theory of *Dharma-śāstra*, the king is not only the head of the civil administration and the fountain of justice, but he is also the final controlling authority in preserving religious and spiritual institutions, he is to see that people follow the dharma, to punish them for breaches of the religious and spiritual codes and to see to the administration to them of appropriate penances. In short, he is also the Defender of the Faith.

But he regulated spiritual and religious matters not by his arbitrary authority but on the advice of his purohit and ministers and after taking the opinion of the assemblies (*pariṣad*) of learned men. Whenever difficult questions arose about the validity of anything from the religious point of view or about penances for lapses, or about excommunicating or outcasting a man, the opinion of the assembly of learned men was sought. Therefore, detailed rules are laid down in the *Dharma-sūtras* and *smritis* about the constitution of *parishads*.

A few words must be said about the pariṣad and about the claims of the Śaṅkarācaryas (the modern heads of *maṭhas*) to regulate religious matters affecting their followers. Among the oldest texts on this point is the one contained in the Taireeya Upanishat (1.11.) viz. the exhortation of the teacher on the eve of the student's departure at the close of his studies.

If you have hereafter a doubt about any rite or about a course of conduct, you should behave in the way in which the brahmins of your place, who are thoughtful, intent (upon doing their duties), act spontaneously (without being urged by any one), are not hard-hearted and have an eye only to dharma (and not to Kama or artha) will behave. The same holds good about your conduct towards persons charged (generally falsely) with sins or lapses".

The words *'Sabha'* (Rig X.34.6) and *'samiti'* (Rig X.97.6) occur even in the Rig Veda but their exact significance is doubtful and the former word at least seems to bear the sense of "gambling hall" in some passages. In the *Upaṇiṣats*, however, the words *samiti* and *pariṣad* assume a more definite sense, meaning 'an assembly of learned men in a particular locality.

The Chandokya Upanishat V.3.1 states that *Śvetaketu Aruṇeya* repaired to the assembly (*samiti*) of the *Pañcālas* (where Pravahana Jaivali put him five questions of a metaphysical and esoteric nature). The Brahadayaranya Upanishat (VI.2.1) when narrating the same episode employs the word *pariṣad*. These passages establish that in the times of the Upaniṣats there were assemblies of learned men where intricate questions were discussed. Gautama prescribes just as the Taitreeya Upanishat (1.11) does that in matters about which there is no certain rule (or there is doubt) one should do what is commended by respectable persons not less than ten in number, who are clever in discussion and are above covetousness. The *Āpastamba Dharma Sutra* (I.3.11.34) declares that holidays other than those stated by him may be observed as settled by parishads.

The *Boudhayana Dharma Sutra* (II.1.41-45) prescribes — "The relatives of a brahmacārī who is guilty of sexual intercourse should empty a water pot in the pariṣad and the offender should confess –

I, so and so by name, am guilty of such and such a misdeed and that after the erring person has performed penance and when he has touched water, milk, ghee, honey and salt, the brahmins should ask him "have you performed the penance?"

The other shall then reply 'yes'; then they shall admit him who has performed penance to all sacrificial rites making no difference between him and others.

This clearly establishes that at least five centuries before the Christian era it was the privilege of the assembly of the learned brahmins to administer penance to a sinner and then restore him to all rights of inter-dining and other social intercourse. *Vasishta Dharma Sutra* (1.16) declares —

There is no doubt that whatever persons who have studied *Dharma-shastra* and the three *Vedas* expound as purifying themselves and others is the proper dharma.

Āpastamba Dharma Sutra (1.1.1.2) declares that the conventions of those that know dharma are the authoritative standard (of conduct for ordinary men). When the *smritis* declare that Veda, smriti and the usages of *śiṣṭas* are the three sources of dharma (e. g. *Vasishta Dharma Sutra* I. 4-5) they convey that *śiṣṭas* can and should determine from time to time what is religious conduct. When Brihaspati enjoins that doubts about dharma should not be settled by blindly following the letter of sastras, but that logic and reasoning should be employed, he strikes the true note of the spirit of the ancient sages.

Manu XII. 108 states — If one were to ask how one should act in matters of dharma on which no express rule is declared in this work, the reply is that in such cases what is declared to be a proper rule of conduct by respectable (*śiṣṭa*) brahmins would undoubtedly be the dharma.

Yājnavalkeeyam (III.300) requires that a person guilty of a sin or lapse should declare it to an assembly of learned brahmins and undergo such *vrata* (penance and observances) as is approved of by the pariṣad. *Śaṅkarācārya* in his *bhāṣya* on Brahadaranyaka Upanishat (IV.3.2) makes the very significant remark —

It is therefore that in coming to a decision on a subtle point of dharma, it is desirable to have a *pariṣad* working and a specially distinguished person is wanted (to give the lead) as stated in the rule "a pariṣad should consist of not less than ten persons or of three or of one (specially distinguished)".

These several authorities establish that for over 1500 years before the great *Śaṅkarācārya* the *pariṣad* of learned brahmins was the acknowledged authority for settling doubtful points of dharma and administering penances on lapses from proper conduct and that *Śaṅkarācārya* himself acknowledged this privilege of the *pariṣad*.

The next question is— what is the number of persons required to constitute a pariṣad for deciding on doubtful points of dharma and what their qualifications should be. According to Gautama (28.46-47) a *pariṣad* should consist of at least ten persons viz. four, each of whom has mastered one Veda, three members who are respectively a (perpetual) student, a house-holder and a *sanyasi* and three more each of whom has studied distinct Dharma-sastras.

Vasishta Dharma Sutra (III.20), Boudayana (1. 1. 8), Parāsara (VIII.27) and *Angirasa* declare that four persons each of whom has mastered one of the four *Vedas*, one who knows the *Mīmāṃsā*, one who has studied the six subsidiary lores of the Veda, one who has studied Dharma-sastra and three persons who are a house-holder, a forest hermit and a *sanyasi* constitute a pariṣad of ten.

Manu IXII.111) defines the ten as consisting of three masters of each of the three *Vedas* (excluding the *Atharva-Veda*), one who has studied Logic, a student of *Mīmāṃsa*, a student of *Nirukta*, a master of *Dharma-sastras* and three members in each of the first three *āśramas*. *Brihaspati* declares that a pariṣad may be constituted by seven or five persons sitting together who have studied the Vedas, their six subsidiary lores and dharma-sastra and that such a pariṣad resembles a solemn sacrifice.

Vasishta Dharma Sutra (III.7), Yājnavalkeeyam (1.9), *Manu* (XII.112), *Parāśara* VIII.11 state that at least four or three men should constitute a pariṣad, but they should be students of each of the four Vedas, should be *agnihotṛis* and should have also studied *dharma-sastra*.

If even three cannot be found then even a single man can declare the dharma in case of doubt (Gautama 28.48), but he must possess special qualifications. Gautama 28. 48, *Manu* XII. 113 (= Atri 143) require that he must be the best of brahmins, a *śiṣṭa* and a deep student of the Veda.

Yājnavalkeeyam (I.9), *Parasara* (VIII.13), Angiras say that a single person who is the best among ascetics possessing knowledge of the Self may form a pariṣad and declare what the proper rule is on a point of doubt. Though the texts permit in extreme cases a single man to declare dharma in case of doubt they give emphatic warning that this should not be done as far as possible. *Boudhayana Dharma Sutra* (I.13) observes — The way of dharma is very subtle and difficult to follow and it has many entrances (i.e. it appears different in different circumstances); therefore, a person though knowing much should not undertake single-handed to propound the proper course of conduct in case of doubt.

The texts also emphasize that doubtful points of dharma are not to be decided by the votes of ignorant people, even if they muster in thousands.

Smṛtikāras state — Even if thousands of brahmins who have observed no vrata and who have studied no Vedic mantras and who make their living merely by virtue of their caste come together they do not constitute a pariṣad. When such foolish persons deluded by ignorance and ignorant of dharma declare (a penance for a sin) the sin is multiplied a hundred-fold and reaches the propounders.

The *Maitreyi* on Yājnavalkeeya (III.300) remarks that the number mentioned as constituting a pariṣad is not material, that all that is meant is that for lesser sins a small number of learned men can declare the penance, but in the case of serious sins, the number of persons who constitute the pariṣad should be large. Devala quoted in the Yājnavalkeeyam (III.300) says that when the sin is not grave, brahmins may declare the penance without reference to the king (and restore the sinner to his privileges) but when the sin is grave, then the king and brahmins must carefully examine the matter and then declare the penance.

Parasara (VIII. 28-29) ordains — Brahmins should declare penance for sins with the king's consent, that they should not declare the expiation of sins by penance of their own motion and that if the king decides to give prāyaścitta without reference to brahmins, the sin becomes increased a hundred-fold.

It is the duty of the pariṣad to declare an appropriate penance when a man comes to it, declares his lapse and seeks to be freed from the taint and if the pariṣad knowing what the appropriate penance is refuses to administer it, they incur the same sin as that committed by the man who approaches them.

Parašara VIII.2 prescribes that one should on being convinced of his having committed a sin at once repair to the assembly of learned men, should prostrate himself on the ground before them and request them to administer prāyaścitta (expiation).

A large part of Northern India was under Moslem rule for about 500 years from about 1200 C.E. and a portion of the Deccan and a part of South India also were under Moslem rule for about 300years. Numerous documents have been published by the late Mr. Vishwanath K. Raj Wade (a scholar, who made unique contributions to the elucidation of Maratha History, Marathi Philology and Marathi Literature) and his friends. From these it appears that during the time of the Maratha domination learned brahmins of holy places like Paithan, Nasik and Karad were consulted in religious matters by the king or his minister, that the holders of the '*gādi* of Śaṅkarācārya at Sankeśvara and Karavīra and other seats were also rarely consulted in these matters and that it is only after the advent of the British rule that the Śaṅkarācāryas have begun to claim almost exclusive jurisdiction in ecclesiastic matters and in restoring men to their castes or excommunicating them for lapses. It will be seen from passages quoted below that both the learned brahmins at holy places like Karad and the Śaṅkarācāryas claim the exclusive right in these matters by reason of immemorial usage.

In several works it is said that the pariṣad must be constituted by śiṣṭas (vide Gautama 28.46). Śiṣṭa is variously defined by some smriti works. The *Boudayana Dharma Sutra* (I.1.5-6) says — Śiṣṭas are those who are free from envy and pride, who keep only as much corn as is measured by *kumbhī*, who are free from greed and from hypocrisy, arrogance, covetousness, delusions and anger. Those are śiṣṭas who have studied the Veda according to the prescribed method, together with its appendages (viz. Itihāsa and Puranas), who know how to draw inferences from that and who tend to make people realize the teaching of the Veda.

The *Mahābhāsya* defines śiṣṭas in almost the same words as *Boudayana Dharma Sutra* 1.1.5. *Vasishta Dharma Sutra* 1.6 defines śiṣṭa as one whose mind is free from desires.

Manu (VI.38,43) & *Aapastambar* (I.9-21.10) – He should neither kindle srauta fires nor *gṛhya* fire nor even ordinary fire for cooking food and should subsist on food obtained by begging.

Goutamar (III.13 & 20) & *Manu* (VI.43,55) – He may enter a village for begging food only once a day, he should not ordinarily stay in a village at night (except in the rains) but if he stays at all he should do so only for one night.

He should beg alms from seven houses without selecting them beforehand. *Boudhayana Dharma Sutra* (II. 10. 57-58) prescribes that he should visit for alms the houses of brahmin householders of the *Śālina* and *Yāyāvara* types and should only wait for as much time as would be required for milking a cow. *Boudhayana Dharma Sutra* II.10.69 quotes the view of others that an ascetic may take alms from persons of all *varnas* or food from only one among *dvijātis*; *Vasishta* (X.24) also says that he should beg of brahmins only. The *Vayu Purāṇa* 1.18.17 prescribes that ascetics should not eat food belonging to one man (but should eat food collected from several houses), or flesh or honey and should not accept *āma-śrāddha* (i.e. *śrāddha* with uncooked food), should not use salt directly or by itself (i.e. they may eat vegetables in cooking which salt has been used).

According to *Uśānas* food obtained by begging is of five kinds viz.;

- *Madhukara* (collecting food from any three, five or seven houses at random just as bees collect honey from any flowers),
- *Prāk-praṇīta* (when a request is made by devotees to take food at their houses even before the ascetic gets up from his bed),
- *Ayācita* (when invitation to take food at his house is given by a man before the ascetic starts on his begging round),
- *Tat-kālika* (the food that is announced by a brahmin the moment the ascetic approaches),
- *Upapanna* (cooked food brought to the math by devoted disciples or other people).

Manu (VI.56) - He should go out for begging when the smoke from kitchens has ceased to rise and when the noise of pestles has died down and the live coals (in the kitchen) have been extinguished and the plates used for the dining (by the householders) have been kept aside i.e. he should beg food in the evening. He should not take as alms honey or flesh (*Vasishta* X.24). He should not endeavour to secure alms by the practice of predicting, interpreting portents and omens or by the practice of describing the consequences indicated by them, nor by astrology nor by expounding the principles of a lore nor by casuistry (or discussion) nor should he approach a house that is already besieged by hermits, brahmins, birds and dogs, beggars or others (*Manu* VI. 50-51).

Manu (VI.57&59) - Taking an additional, bowl, staff or similar artefact for future use is "accumulation of possessions".

He should wear garments only for covering his private parts and may wear such garments as were worn by others and are used by him after washing (Gautama III.17-18), while *Āpastamba Dharma Sutra* (II. 9. 21. 11-12) states that he should wear clothes thrown away by others and that some say that he may be naked. Vasishta (X. 9-11) says that he should cover his body with a piece of cloth (*śāṭi*) or with deer skin or with grass cut down for cows. *Boudhayana Dharma Sutra* II.6.24 requires that his garments should be ochre-coloured (quoted by *Aparārka*).

The begging bowl and the plate from which the ascetic eats should be made of clay or wood or of a gourd, or of bamboo which should be without holes and he should not use metal vessels; and these vessels are to be cleaned, with water and scoured with cow's hair.

Manu (VI.52) – He should pare his nails, cut all his hair and beard; but Gautama (III.21) appears to allow him an option viz. he may tonsure the whole head or keep only a top-knot.

Manu (VI.43) – He should sleep on raised ground (sthaṇḍila), should feel no concern if he suffers from an illness, he should neither welcome death nor should he feel joy for continuing to live, but he should patiently wait till the time of death, as a servant waits till the time he is hired expires.

Manu (VI.43) - He should generally observe silence except when he repeats the Vedic texts learnt by him. He should recite the Vedic texts referring to yajñas or gods or texts of a metaphysical character found in the Vedānta (such as *"satyam jñānam-anantam brahma"* in Taitreeya Upanishat 2.1).

Aapastamba referring the *Bouddhayana Dharma Sutra* says - - He should not eat food to satiety, but should eat only as much as is necessary to keep body and spirit together and should not feel delight when he gets substantial alms nor feel dejected when he gets little or nothing.

There is a famous verse — An ascetic should take only eight morsels of food, a forest hermit, a householder 32 and a Vedic student an unlimited number.

Vayu Puranam (I.8) - He should hoard nothing and he should own or possess nothing except his tattered garments, his water jar, begging bowl. Devala quoted by the Maitrayana on Yājnavalkeeya (III.58) declares that the ascetic should possess only a water-jar, a Pavitra (cloth for straining water), pādukās, (wooden clogs) an āsana (a seat) and a kanthā (patched blanket for protection from extreme cold). The Mahabharata states that wearing ochre-coloured garments, shaving the head and keeping a water jar and three staffs these are only outward signs meant to secure food and do not lead to *moksha* (dialogue of *Janaka* and *Sulabha*).

The *Vayu Purāṇa* I.8 (quoted by Aparārka) lays down what he should possess. He should take a staff of bamboo the outward surface of which is intact, which is not formidable and which has the parvans (the parts between the joints) of equal length, which is surrounded by a rope of cow's tail hair four inches (aṅgulas) in length and has three knots and which he holds in his right hand; he should have a śikya (loop on which to carry his jar or other things) made of kuśa or cotton or hemp threads or strings and of the form of a lotus and six muṣṭis (fists) in length; he should also have a water jar and a pātra (vessel or bowl for begging); he may have a seat (āsana) of wood square or round in size for sitting on or for washing his feet; he should have a loin- cloth to cover his private parts and a kanthā (patched garment) for protection against cold and he may have two pādukas (sandals). He should have only these and should not accumulate anything else.

It is well-known that Shivaji, the great founder of the Maratha Empire, established a council of eight ministers, viz. Mukhya Pradhāna, Āmatya, Saciva, Mantrī, Senāpati, Paṇḍita-rao, Nyāyadhīsa and Sumanta. The jurisdiction of the Paṇḍita-rao extended over all religious matters, he was to examine and decide disputes about dharma and adharma, he was to honour śiṣṭas (respectable people) on behalf of the king, was to make his signature expressing his approval of the writings (decisions) about *ācāra*, *vyavahāra* and *prāyaścittas* (made by learned brahmins). He was to superintend and carry into immediate execution gifts, propitiatory rites (for the king).

We see that asceticism presents several aspects viz. fasting or at least reducing the intake of food, abstention from meat and drink and pleasures of sense, total absence of sexual gratification and suppression of the sexual emotion, vow of silence, sleeping on bare ground, nakedness or making use of minimum clothing, contempt for the world and its riches.

The Hindu Scriptures however do not enjoin self-infliction of pain or flagellation that was indulged in by monks in the early centuries of Christianity. Asceticism in the several forms indicated above is a feature common to all religions. It is the fashion to assert that Indians have the highest regard for asceticism and that the men whose memories they cherish as ideals of human conduct are ascetics.

Some of the duties of the *Sanyasis* are mentioned in this book more than once or in more than one chapter. They are just to stress and also to emphasize that the same has been conveyed by more than one text or sage.

Sannyasa Dharmam

दुर्वृत्तोवा सुवृत्तोवा मूर्ख: पण्डित एव वा काषाय दण्ड मात्रेण यति: पूज्य: नसंशय:

Durvruttō Vā Suvruttō Vā Mūrkka: Paṇḏita Ēva Vā
Kāṣāya Daṇḏa Mātrēṇa Yatiḥ Pūjyō Na Samśayaḥ
Neeti Shastram

Whether the person was good or bad or intelligent or idiot, just because he wears a saffron dress and has a staff (*Dandam*) on hand he becomes worthy of *pujas* – i.e. just any *sanyasi* is worshippable. His background should not be verified.

In Hinduism, asceticism, denotes reducing the desires. It you to do the housework properly. *Thirugnaana Sambandar* also has sung that he was happy to see God as Goddess in the *Thevaram* song "*Peṇṇil Nallāḷōṭum Peruntakai Iruntatē*".

There are many *Vedic* and *Shastra* texts on *Sannyasa Dharma*. Let us try to understand some of them.

Texts on *Sanyasam*

Adi Shankara's Gita Bhashyam explains the sannyasa dharma and methods in detail.

There are many *Upanishats* to explain *sannyasa dharma*. They are;

#	***Upanishat***	***Veda***
1.	*Matāmnāya Upanishat*	*Rig*
2.	*Nirvāṇa Upanishat*	
3.	*Aruṇeya (Aruṇī) Upanishat*	*Sāma*
4.	*Maitreya Upanishat*	
5.	*Maitrāyaṇī Upanishat*	
6.	*Aruṇeya (Aruṇī) Upanishat*	
7.	*Saṉyāsa (Bruhat Saṉyāsa) Upaniṣat*	
8.	*Kuṇṭika Upaniṣat*	
9.	*Bahma Upaniṣat*	*Krişṇa Yajur*

#	*Upanishat*	*Veda*
10.	*Avatūta(ka) Upaniṣat*	
11.	*Kaṭaśruti (Kaṭa Rudra) Upaniṣat*	
12.	*Jābāla Upaniṣat*	*Śukla Yajur*
13.	*Paramahamsa Upaniṣat*	
14.	*Advayatāraka Upaniṣat*	
15.	*Bikṣuka Upaniṣat*	
16.	*Turiyātītavadūta Upaniṣat*	
17.	*Yākñavalkya Upaniṣat*	
18.	*Śatavaṉīya Upaniṣat*	
19.	*Āśrama Upaniṣat*	*Atharva*
20.	*Nāradaparivrājaka Upaniṣat*	
21.	*Paramahamsa Parivrājaka Upaniṣat*	
22.	*Parabrahma Upaniṣat*	

Some of the oldest *Sannyasa Upanishats* have a strong *Advaita Vedanta* perspective and all of these predate Adi Shankara. Most of the *Sannyasa Upanishats* put forward the philosophies of *Yoga* and *Advaita*. The reason for this is that the major Hindu monasteries of the early and medieval times (first millennium C.E.) followed the *Advaita* Vedanta tradition.

These texts are influential and often discussed by medieval Indian scholars. For example, *Sri Adi Shankara* mentions the *Jaabala Upanishat* in his commentaries on the *Brahma Sutras*.

The 12th century *Shatavaneeya Upanishat* is a notable exception. It puts forward the *Vedanta* philosophies of *Dvaitam* and *Vishishtadvaitam*.

<u>*Sanyasam* in *Dharma Shastras*</u>

Different Rishis have defined *sannyasa dharma* in *Dharma Shastras*. Let us look at them a bit;

1. <u>*Angirasa*</u> Says – Asceticism can be attained only when apathy arises in all things. If *sanyasam* is taken without *vairagya*, he will become a waste.

Yatā Maṉasi Sañjātam Vaidruṣṇyam Sarvavastuṣu |
Tatā Saṉyāsamiccanti Patitasyāt Viparyayē | |

2. Hārīda says – The person who has obtained zealous (*Vairagyam*) must obtain asceticism. The person who is interested on worldly matters is *Grahastan* and he has to perform *karmas* is the right method. If the devotee who has attachment in worldly matters takes asceticism, he will reach the hell.

Viraktaḥ Pravrajētīmāṉ Samraktastu Gruhēvasēt |
Sarāgō Narakam Yāti Pravrajaṉ Hi Dvijādamaḥ ||

3. *Jabala shruti* talks about *Ashrama Samuccchayam* – If zeal does not come while in the respective *ashrams*, then one should accept all the three *ashrams* and then attain asceticism by acquiring zeal. When the zeal is strong in any *ashram*, one can attain sannyasa directly without going to the next ashram(s). Therefore, it is said that the obtaining *Sannyasa* is entirely dependent on *vairagya*.

In order to generate the feeling of *vairagya* (desire-lessness) and to curb his senses he should make his mind dwell upon the body as liable to disease and old age and as packed full of impurities; and should revolve in his mind the transitory nature of all mundane things, the trouble one has to undergo in body and mind from conception to death, the incessant round of births and deaths.

Brahmacaryam Samāpya Gruhībavēt Gruhībūtvā Vaṉī Bavēt Vaṉī Būtvā Pravrajētyati Vēta Ratā Brahmacaryādēva Pravrajēt Gruhātvā Vaṉādvā

4. Yama says – The sins generated through generations are burnt by the sannyasam like the husky-fire purifies the gold.

Yē Ca Santāṉajā Dōṣāḥ Yē Ca Syuḥ Karmasambavāḥ |
Saṉyāsastāṉ Dahēt Sarvām Stuṣāgṉiriva Kāñcaṉam ||

5. Vyasa says – Lord Vasudevan has two forms - one form is *sanyasi* and the other a *Pratima* form; The sannyasa form is wandering and the *Pratima* form is static.

Dvērūpē Vāsudēvasya Caramca Acaramēva Ca |
Caram Sanyāsinām Rūpam Acalam Pratimātikam ||

Any Brahmin who duly practices sannyasa, the essence of *Moksha* and practices it with austerities, attains the form of *Brahmam* as the gentle *Agni*.

Mōkṣāśramam Yaścarate Yatōktam Śucis'su Samkalpita Buddhiiyuktaḥ |
Anintanam Jyōtiriva Praśāntam Sabrahmabhāvam Vrajatē Dvijātiḥ ||

6. Daksha says – The one who has attained asceticism saves all the 30 generations of *Pitrus* before him and the 30 generations of Pitrus after him – thus all the Pitrus before and after him from Hell as soon as he acquires *Sannyasa*.

Trimśatparām Strimśadaparān Trimśacca Prataḥ Pradhān |
Satyascanyasanādēva Narakātrāyatē Pitrūn ||

7. Samvartta says – The *Bhikshus* are divided into four divisions - the *Kuteechaakar*, the *Bahootakar*, the *Hamsar* and the *Paramahamsar*[12]. The latter one is superior to the earlier ones.

Caturvitābikṣanastu Kuṭīcaka Bahūtakou |
Hamsaḥ Paramahamsaśca Yōyaḥ Paśvāt Sa Uttamaḥ ||

8. Bodhaayana says – The *Kuteecaka sanyasi*, after obtaining Sanyasam, should take food in his or his relatives house. He should have tuft, holy thread, three *dandams* and water-pot. He should continue to do *Gayatri japam* regularly.

Kuṭīcakastu Sanyasya Svīyavēśmani Nityaśaḥ
Bikṣāmādāya Buñjīta Svabandūnām Gruhī'Stavā |
Śikāyajñōpavītī Syāt Tridaṇḍī Sakamaṇṭaluḥ ||
Sāvitrīm Sahasra Krutva Āvartayēt Śatakrutvō'Sparamita Krutvōvā ||

[12] These type of divisions in Sanyasam has been discussed in detail in a different chapter.

Other than the *Anushtana* period, he has to continue the japa, meditation, reading/ hearing the *puranas* like *Bhagavatam/ Ramayana* etc. Lord should be meditated upon always in the lotus heart.

Japadyāṉētihāsaiśca Diṉaśēṣam Nayētbhutaḥ |
Hrutpuṇṭarīkanilayam Dyāyēt Ātmāṉam Avyayam ||

A *Bahootakar sanyasi* should sacrifice all the relations and take alms from non-relative houses. No more than seven homes, at a time, should be taken. He should not take further, if enough is available in two or three houses. In the remaining areas he should practice as a *Kuteecaka*.

Bahūtakastu Saṉyasya Bantuputrādivarjitaḥ |
Saptāgāram Carētbaikṣam Ēkāṉṉam Ca Parityajēt ||

9. Vishnu says – *Hamsa sanyasi* can have only the things – one *yagnopaveetam*, a single *dandam*, a saffron garment, a comfortable garment to move the insects on the earth (for the *ahimsa* purposes). The remaining things are the same as before.

Yagñōpavītam Daṇḏam Ca Vastram Jantu Nivāraṇam |
Tāvat Parigrahaḥ Prōktaḥ Nāṉyō Hamsa Parigrahaḥ ||

Elderly and sick monks can live in one place in the city or in a comfortable village, depending on the time period. There is nothing wrong in this. They should be specially cared, serviced and worshiped by the *grahastras*.

Vruddhāṉāmadhurāṇām Ca Bikṣūṇām Saṅgavarjiṇām |
Grāmēvāta Purē Vāpi Vāsō Naikatra Tiṣṭati ||

10. Sage *Atri* says – *Paramahamsa sanyasi* can have only two loincloths, a torn-out blanket and a *dandam*. A water pot is a must. Meditating on *Brahmam* should be done by suppressing the mind and other senses. Always keep doing *Pranav japam*. Vedanta should be heard (*shravanam*) practiced in mind (*mananam*) and *nididhyasanam*. Swayam should be considered as the form of *Vishnu*, with the intention of "*Ātmā Ēkaḥ*". He can live in a clean place anywhere.

Koupīṉayugalam Kantādaṇḏa Ēkaḥ Parigrahaḥ |
Yatēḥ Paramahamsasya Nādikantu Vidīyatē |
Paraḥ Paramahamsastu Turyākyaḥ Śruti Śāsanāt |
Dāntaḥ Śāntaḥ Satvasamaḥ Praṇavābyāsa Taptaraḥ ||
Śravaṇādirataśśuddhaḥ Nididhyāsaṉataptaraḥ ||
Brahmabhāvēṉa Sampūrya Brahmāṇḏamakilam Stitaḥ |
Ātmatruptaścātmaratiḥ Sa Malōṣṭāśma Kāñcaṉaḥ ||
Tatvam Padaika Bōdācca Viṣṇu Rūpaḥ Svayamsadhā ||
Nivasēparamahamsastuyatra Kvāpi Katañcaṉa ||

11. _Paraasara_ says – Let lust, anger, arrogance, greed and stupidity go off and be free from arrogance.

Kāmam Krōdam, Tatā Darpam Lōbamōhādayaśca Yēdāstu |
Dōṣāṉ Parityajya Parivrāt Nirmamō Bavēt ||

12. _Bhavishya Puranam_ says – The qualifications of a *Daṇḏam* is – should be of bamboo, beautiful, leathery, even number knotted, has many a black dot (sign of completion), with no branches, straight, sprouting from the ground, up to the nose/ eyebrows. Such a staff should be worn by the *sanyasi*.

Daṇḏam Tu Vaiṇavam Soumyam Satvacam Samaparvakam |
Puṇya Stāṉasamutpaṉṉam Nāṉākalmāpa Śopitam ||
Adagda Mahatam Gīṭai: Parvagranti Virājitam |
Swayam Bhūtēntumēdiṉyām Śākāvarjamrujum Śubham |
Nāsādagṉam Śirōdastu Bruvōrvā Bibruyāditi ||

13. _Yagnavalkaya_ says – The Vedanta book can be obtained from the householder, if there is a desire.

Adhyātma Pustakam Viprair Dattam Gruhīta Bikṣukaḥ ||

Always should be alone. The optimal answer to the question should be with '*Narayana*' sound. Should not talk unnecessarily.

Ēkākī Nispruhastiṣṭaṉ Na Kēṉāpi Sahāvasēt |

Dadyāṉ Nārāyaṇētyēva Prati Vākyam Sadāyatiḥ ||

Meditation, cleanliness, begging and being always alone, are the only four activities for a *Paramahamsa* and does not have a fifth one.

Dyāṉam Śaucam Tatābikṣā Nityamēkānta Śīlatā |
Bikṣāḥ Catvāri Karmāṇi Pañcamam Nōpapadyatē ||

Paramahamsa should perform *Harihara* Puja. But he should not pinch basil, etc., from the plants. He should worship with fallen petals. *Moksha* will be given by *Vishnu* and wisdom by *Parameswara*.

Swayam Patita Tulasī Patrādyaiḥ Svayamāhrutaiḥ |
Pūjayēṉ Mōkṣatam Viṣṇum Kñāṉatam Ca Mahēśvaram ||

14. Sage *Kanva* says – He can stay, for one night in a village, five nights in a city and four months in a comfortable place during the rainy season.

Ēkarātram Vasēt Grāmē Nagarē Pañca Rātrakam |
Varṣāpyōṅsyatra Varṣāsu Māsāmśca Caturō Vasēt ||

15. *Manu* (6:35) says – Some important qualifications to become a *Sanyasi*;

Only after paying his three debts[13] should a man set his mind on renunciation. Should he take to renunciation without paying them he will fall.

Some teachers on the other hand say that one may depart for the mendicant's life immediately after completing study. Some teachers also recommend that the blind and handicapped should also renounce early. If a person has chronic ailment or is facing an imminent death then he too may renounce.

[13] The three debts and their repayment are — to the gods — through yajñas, to the *rishis* through study & teaching and to the ancestors through procreation.

A man should renounce, therefore only after he has examined the purity of his heart for a long time and ascertained that his mind will not waive from *Dharma*.

16. *Angirasa* says – A *sanyasi* should have a sacrificial thread, a triple staff (*dandam*), a cloth to strain insects, a sling, a begging bowl, a stool (*kurmāsana*), a loincloth and a waist-band. Only a man who possesses these is a true ascetic. (*Yati dharma samuccaya* 5:15-16)

17. *Galava* says – Now a wandering ascetic bears the insignia: is shaven-headed, or wears a *śikha*, a sacrificial thread, dons a ragged ochre garment9. Let him wear a cloth to cover his loins but no upper garment. He carries a triple-staff, a water-strainer, a water-pot, a bowl and a ragged blanket. (*Yati dharma samuccaya* 5:219)

18. *Kratu* says – He may carry 10 or 20 articles or at least 5. A ragged shawl, a needle & thread, a deer-skin, an umbrella, water-strainer, water-pot, stool, bowl, sling, rosary, sacrificial thread, a spade, a pair of sandals, loincloth, tripod, a pair of shoes, a staff, a yoga-band and an outer-garment. Of these 20 only 5 are obligatory — sacrificial thread, triple-staff, water-strainer, bowl, loincloth and waist-band. (*Yati dharma samuccaya* 5:26)

19. *Brihaspati* says – He should wear a loin-cloth. According to some he should use discarded clothes after washing them. (*Yati dharma samuccaya* 3:18-19)

20. *Hārita* says – He should wear a loin cloth and a blanket/ shawl as protection against the cold and a pair of sandals. Let him not take possession of anything else.

21. *Śankha* says – He should carry in his hand the triple-staff tied with the water strainer and wear a garment made of grass, ragged (or rough) cloth, or tree bark and have one change of clothes. Some permit also a blanket against the cold.

22. *Gerua* says – Even though the term ochre is used without further specification, nevertheless one should colour the garments with red-chalk known as *gairika* (*Yati dharma samuccaya* 8:64).

23. *Śaunaka* says – Ten vows are enjoined on all ascetics — non-injury, telling the truth, honesty, chastity, poverty, suppression of anger, obedience to the teacher, cleanliness, refraining from wrongful conduct in mental, verbal and physical activities and to avoid carelessness. (*Yati dharma samuccaya* 5:56 - 57).

24. *Bodhāyana* says – Now then these are the vows: non-injury, telling the truth, honesty, chastity and renunciation (of all possessions). These are the secondary vows: suppression of anger, obedient service to the teacher, avoiding carelessness, cleanliness and purity of food. (*Bruhadaaranyaka Upanishat* 2:18.2-3).

Every *sanyasi* must be held accountable by his disciples for these common vows—

24.1. Non-violence (*ahimsa*) – Since there are different types of injury, we must undoubtedly distinguish different types of non-injury. (*Yati dharma samuccaya* 5:62)

Now there are ten types of injury from which a *sanyasi* must refrain—

24.1.1 Causing anxiety (mental pain)
24.1.2 Causing physical pain
24.1.3 Causing someone to weep,
24.1.4 Drawing blood
24.1.5 Calumny — the making of false and defamatory statements about someone in order to damage their reputation; slander.

24.1.6 Destroying someone's happiness,
24.1.7 Conquest — engaging in the take-over of another enterprise.
24.1.8 Making someone grovel — humiliating someone.
24.1.9 Obstructing someone's welfare — either through acts or endorsements or proclamations or encouragements
24.1.10 Killing any living being. (Some include even plants in this prohibition).

24.2. Speaking the truth — a *sanyasi* should always speak the truth but should also speak only beneficial truth, speech that is directed at improving or teaching another.

24.3. Honesty — a *sanyasi* should never engage in any type of fraud or duplicitous dealings and all times and places obey the law of the land.

24.4. Chastity — a *sanyasi* must completely refrain from all forms of sexual activity. Different types of sexual activity—

24.4.1 To think fondly of previous sexual activity.
24.4.2 To tell someone about previous sexual acts.
24.4.3 To engage in any form of flirtatious activity.
24.4.4 To look at an attractive person in an admiring and lustful way.

24.4.5 To speak in secret to an attractive person i.e. to invite an attractive person into one's room or any other private or secluded space. i.e. a *sanyasi* should never be alone in a room with a young person.
24.4.6 To formulate an intention to seduce someone.
24.4.7 To make a resolve and plan a sexual act — inducing another to act as a go-between.
24.4.8 To actually engage in a sexual act.

All these are the 8 types of sexual activity according to Brihaspati. Their opposite is what is called chastity. (5:66-67)

If a *sanyasi* continues to engage in sexual activity he will be born as a beetle living in dung for 60,000 years. Thereafter he will be born as a mouse living in abandoned houses. And then he will be reborn as a dog for 12 lifetimes, then he will become a vulture for 20 years and a pig for 9 years (*Shatapata Brahmanam*).

This hyperbole is meant to stress how disgraceful and wrong any sexual activity is after taking *Sannyasa*.

24.5 Renunciation of possessions — a *sanyasi* should not accumulate any possession, not even the permitted articles of an ascetic for use at a future date. In other words when an article becomes unusable than another of the same sort can be resourced. (*Yati dharma samuccaya* 5:68)

24.6. Suppression of anger — a *sanyasi* should make every effort not to become angry for any reason whatsoever. Anger-management is one of the foremost activities of a *sanyasi.*

24.7. Obedience to the guru — a *sanyasi* should obey the initiating (*deekṣa*) guru or abbot (*mahānta*) of the monastery (*aśrama*) in every respect, except if commanded to do something illegal or to act contrary to the dictates of the śāstra or to break a monastic vow.

24.8. Cleanliness — a *sanyasi* should bathe at regular times[14] and maintain optimum hygiene – brushing the teeth regularly, keeping the nails and hair/beard trimmed and neat. A *sanyasi* must also maintain the cleanliness and tidiness of his bedding and *kuṭir* (cell).

24.9. Mindfulness — a *sanyasi* must strenuously avoid all acts of negligence and must be mindful of his every act, understanding that he is an exemplar of the Dharma and a role model for others.

24.10 Abstaining from wrongful conduct — a *sanyasi* must avoid causing harm, injury or pain to any living being by mental, verbal or physical means.

24.11. Purity of food. — a *sanyasi* should preferably obtain his one meal a day by begging. If he is living in an *aśrama* (monastery) then he should ensure that the food that is served is pure and ethically obtained. Some authorities would argue that this is not a vow as such because it would be hard to maintain with frequent infractions.

25. *Manu Dharma Sutram* Chapter 6 imposes these conditions to a *Sanyasi*;

25.1 A *sanyasi* must relinquish all property.

25.2 A *sanyasi* must give a promise of safety to all beings — whatever being comes to the *sanyasi* for refuge he is under an obligation to give it.

---

[14] Traditionally a *sanyasi* is expected to take bath three times a day. But it has to be seen whether this practical in the current environment – all the times and all the places.

25.3 A *sanyasi* must abstain from injuring creatures; he should not cause the slightest fear to any being.

25.4 A *sanyasi* must practice restraint of the senses, he must entirely abstain from any form of sensual enjoyment — any form of luxury is forbidden. This is socially and cutlery conditioned, but the general guideline is the *sanyasi* must use whatever the lowest socio-economic group in the society in which he is based use for their bedding, accommodation, bathing etc. Traditionally in India a *sanyasi* must always sleep on the ground and never use a bed because the majority of the common people sleep on the floor.

25.5 A *sanyasi* must politely reject all forms of enjoyments that may be offered.

25.6 A *sanyasi* must relinquish love and hatred. He must not bear affection towards favourable people nor malice towards unfavourable people.

25.7 A *sanyasi* must be equal-minded towards all sentient beings. He should not be partial to devotees nor impartial and hostile to any others.

25.8 A *sanyasi* must regularly practice the vow of noble silence (*mouna*). At regular times of periods the *sanyasi* should observe the vow of silence and not speak any words whatsoever.

25.9 A *sanyasi* must patiently bear harsh words that are spoken against him without retaliating. He must never intentionally insult anybody. Against an angry man let him not in return show anger, let him bless when he is cursed and let him never say anything that is devoid of truth.

25.10 A *sanyasi* must speak only the truth — he should not comment on anything that he does not personally know nor speak about things without knowing the established facts.

25.11 A *sanyasi* should always wander alone, without any companion

— nowadays many *sanyasi*s live in *aśrams* or monasteries — this injunction is observed by avoiding the cultivation of friendships with the other monks.

25.12 A *sanyasi* must cultivate indifferent to everything, remain firm of purpose, meditating (and) concentrating his mind on Brahmam.

25.13 Should wear coarse worn-out garments — he should wear simple cotton garments, preferable not stitched, but if the weather conditions do not permit — like in Europe then he should wear the simplest possible garments.

25.14 A *sanyasi* should keep his heart pure — in other words he should cultivate loving kindness and compassion towards all being and repress any unwholesome and negative thinking.

25.15 Let a *sanyasi* avoid creating enemies for the sake of his (perishable) body — a *sanyasi* should never create enmity for the sake of preserving his own body, eating or living arrangements. If his presence in a particular locality causes enmity then he should remove himself to another place.

25.16 A *sanyasi* must not earn a living by (explaining) unusual atmospheric occurrences and omens, nor by practicing astrology and palmistry, nor by giving advice and by the exposition (of the *Shastras*).

A *sanyasi* must not try to interpret dreams, or the sight of comets or hurricanes or interpret birth-charts etc. nor counsel people nor teach the sastras for payment. The only vocation permitted is giving teaching on dharma and expositions of the *Upanishat*s – for this he may accept unsolicited donations but never a fixed salary.

25.17 A *sanyasi* must always have his hair, nails and beard trimmed. Traditionally the head and beard are shaved once a month on the full moon.

25.18 A *sanyasi* should carry an alms-bowl, a staff and a water-pot.

25.19 A *sanyasi* must not use vessels made of metal. The prohibition against a *sanyasi* using metal used to extend also to money and any other item. Nowadays in the west it would be very hard to observe this rule unless a *sanyasi* were to have a credit card — but having a bank-account is forbidden and therefore money has to be used.

25.20 A *sanyasi* must disdain all (food) obtained in consequence of humble salutations. By eating little and by standing and sitting in solitude. He should beg in silence and not be obsequious with the intention of maximizing his alms. The formal request to the mother of the house is— *bhavati bhikṣām dehi* — respect lady please give me alms! No prior salutation or asking after one's health or family is required. The *sanyasi* must eat only once a day.

25.21 A *sanyasi* must not undertake any projects with the intention of acquiring merit. He may engage in projects of social work and relief and engage in projects which benefit the poor, down-trodden, refugees, marginalized members of society etc. but it should be done with disinterest and never for acquiring merit or fame. The *sanyasi*'s name should never be attached to welfare projects.

25.22 A *sanyasi* must dedicate himself to the practice of meditation. The principal religious activity for a *sanyasi* is meditation only. He is forbidden to engage in pujas and yajñas.

25.23 Let him recognize the essential nature of the supreme *Jīva* and its presence in all organisms, both the highest and the lowest. He must practice viewing the *ātman* as pervading all beings, in this way he will be able to cultivate equanimity and equality of vision.

25.24 *Āpastamba* says – A *sanyasi* must live without fire or a house and without comfort or protection.

He must never kindle or touch fire either to cook for himself or to perform oblations. He may dwell in an aśrama but should not dwell in houses. He must avoid comfort using only what is necessary to maintain health — heaters in winter and fans in summer but only as is necessary. He should never take any means of protecting himself from enemies etc.

25.25 A *sanyasi* should not treat people who are sick, poisoned or possessed. A *sanyasi* who has medical knowledge can, in a case of emergency treat patients and all other *sanyasi*s can nurse the sick, lepers etc. as part of their service, but it should never be done for payment.

25.26 A *sanyasi* should not acquire a lot of disciples nor broadcast his knowledge. A *sanyasi* should avoid attracting masses of devotees and followers because of the politics involved which will eventually lead to his being compromised. He should also never advertise his knowledge or competencies and should strive to maintain a low public profile.

25.27 *Kapila* says – A *sanyasi* must refrain from uttering words of greeting or blessing. The usual greeting and blessing of a *sanyasi* is simply to raise his hand in *abhaya mudra* (the gesture of the gift of fearlessness) and utter the name of God such as "*nārāyaṇa nārāyaṇa*".

25.28 *Jamadagni* says – A *sanyasi* should refrain from the use of betel. This would include the use of cigarettes, ganja and any other form of stimulation

25.29 Medhātithi says – A *sanyasi* should refrain from alchemy, judicial litigation, astrology, buying and selling and all crafts. Alchemy would refer to all compounding of any substance whatsoever. A *sanyasi* should avoid all forms of litigation in which he is the plaintiff. All indulgence in astrology and prescribing cures and all forms of trade are forbidden.

25.30 A *sanyasi* should not watch dances and shows, attend gambling events, look at young women, festive foods or menstruating women.

A *sanyasi* should never pass time by watching TV shows or movies nor attend any festive events such as weddings, births etc. Out of courtesy one may invite one's guru who is a *sanyasi* but he should never attend such an event but may send a householder or student as a proxy.

25.31 A *sanyasi* should never live in 6 types of places, royal courts, cities, economic centers, granaries, cattle farms and houses.

25.32 A *sanyasi* should never even think of these 6— selfish-desire, hatred, arrogance, pride, hypocrisy and malice towards others.

25.33 These are the 6 causes of an ascetic's fall: travelling at night, travelling in vehicles, talking about women, greed, sleeping on beds and wearing white clothes.

25.34 These are the 6 causes of a *sanyasi*'s bondage: residence, lack of a begging-bowl, accumulation of possessions, gathering of disciples, sleeping during the day and idle conversation.

25.35 A *sanyasi* should be tongueless, neuter (*kliba*), lame, blind, deaf and stupid.

25.35.1 When a *sanyasi*, as he eats does not notice the difference between tasty and not tasty, whether hot or sweet is called 'tongueless'.

25.35.2 A *sanyasi* unmoved to passion by a 16-year-old young lady, a new born girl and an old woman is called 'neuter'.

25.35.3 A *sanyasi* who walks only to beg food, to answer the calls of nature and does not travel beyond 3 miles is 'lame'.

25.35.4 When a wandering ascetic does not look beyond 6 feet in front of him, unless there is some danger, is said to be 'blind'.

25.35.5 A *sanyasi* who is indifferent to kind or unkind words, praise or abuse is said to be 'deaf'.

25.35.6 When a *sanyasi*, in the presence of hostile people remains silent and acts as if he were asleep even though he has the full use of his faculties is said to be 'stupid'.

25.36 *Kratu* says – By accepting servants, houses, vehicles, cows, real estate, grain, money and gold a *sanyasi* destroys 200 generations of his family. *Sanyasis* who are intent on giving gifts, as well as accumulating clothes and other such goods will end up in a putrid hell because of their stupidity.

25.37 If someone reverts from *Sannyasa* he will be born as a beetle living in dung for 60,000 years. He (becomes an outcaste and) should be excluded from all religious activities.

25.38 *Vasishta* says – Acquiring disciples for profit and self-adulation is the sign of a false ascetic.

26 Conditions for begging;

26.1 A *sanyasi* may go to a village for his daily food. Let him not (in order to beg) go near a house filled with hermits, Brahmanas, birds, dogs, or other mendicants.

Let him go to beg once (a day), let him not be eager to obtain a large quantity (of alms).

26.2 When no smoke ascends from (the kitchen), when the pestle lies motionless, when the embers have been extinguished, when the people have finished their meal, when the dishes have been washed, let the ascetic always go to beg.

26.3 Let him not be sorry when he obtains nothing, nor rejoice when he obtains (something), let him (accept) so much only as will sustain life, let him not care about the (quality of his) utensils.

26.4 A *sanyasi* may go to beg at 3, 5 or 7 houses that have not been previously selected (for the quality of their food).

27 Rules for eating

27.1 A *sanyasi* should not eat a full meal in one house.

27.2 A *sanyasi* may eat a full meal at one house, only if he is old, sick or suffering from a chronic ailment or as an act of kindness (to the host)

27.3 A *sanyasi* should eat only enough to sustain life — eight mouthfuls. A *sanyasi* should avoid eating food that has been offered to ancestors.

27.4 A *sanyasi* should avoid food if accepting it would cause hardship to someone

27.5 *Jaabali* the senior says – a *sanyasi* should not inquire after the donor's class or if state of purity, when the alms-food falls into the bowl let him not think whether it is pure or impure.

27.6 A *sanyasi* should not beg food from families that are related to him. He should eat healthy foods that are easily digested.

27.7 A *sanyasi* should never add salt to the food that is served to him.

Some guidelines for householders (*grahastas*)

1 Do not seek out or prefer to take a *sanyasi* as a guru unless householder gurus are not available.
2 Never physically touch a *sanyasi* — either on the body or the feet, unless compelled to do so during travel etc.
3 It is not advisable to sit on the same bench or seat unless travelling.
4. Never seek blessings from a *sanyasi* — they are not permitted to bless.
5. Never seek personal or domestic advice or counsel from a *sanyasi*.

6. Never discuss your personal or domestic issues with a *sanyasi*.
7. Never offer any personal service to a *sanyasi* such as massaging of the feet, head-rub, shoulder rub, body scrub etc. except in cases of sickness and as treatment only.
8. When organizing travel arrangements, make sure he has a (male) disciple or attendant with him to attend to his needs.
9. One should not book business or first-class travel — the travel arrangements should be the most basic available.
10. When arranging accommodation in houses it is best that the *sanyasi* be housed by several different people during his stay.

11. The *sanyasi* should be given a separate room but no extra luxuries such as soft bedding, pillows, spas, TV or any entertainment should be provided. He should preferably sleep on the floor.
12. If accommodating in a hotel then it should be the most basic motel or hotel. All arrangements should be those that are available to the common people only.
13. Food served should come from 3, 5 or 7 houses and never from one house. So, it is preferable to have 3 or 5 items cooked by different women and served.
14. A *sanyasi* is supposed to eat after every one else has eaten, so always make an attempt to serve him last in a separate area.
15. A *sanyasi* should only eat 8 handfuls of food – so when serving, serve small portions and do not insist that he eat more.

16. A *sanyasi* will eat only once a day so do not make elaborate arrangements for 3 or more meals. If need be some fruit and milk can be offered in the evening.
17. Never present any gift to the *sanyasi* unless it is vitally important for their work or well- being. Especially no luxury item should be gifted such as jewelry, wrist watches or adornments.
18. If a new robe is required it should be made of coarse cotton or hemp and be coloured ochre, never silk.
19. Nowadays most people consider a mobile phone as essential personal equipment — a *sanyasi* may have a phone since a mobile phone has a clock, alarm, calendar, diary etc. Without these accessories travel would be impossible. Other technology would also be useful such as iPads, computers etc.
20. No property may be bequeathed to a *sanyasi* – one may give it to the monastery to be utilized for the benefit of the community but never to individual monks.

21. A *sanyasi* should never be invited to attend dance performances or any form of entertainment — you may extend the courtesy of inviting them to open the proceedings or address such audiences before the performance starts, but make arrangements for them to depart before the performance begins.
22. *Sanyasi* should not be invited to watch secular movies, historical or Dharmic movies are permitted or ones that are useful for social action.

23. *Sanyasi* should never be invited to weddings or birth ceremonies; they may certainly be invited to initiations (upanayanas) and funerals.
24. A woman should never be alone with a *sanyasi* at any time — there is absolutely no reason that a woman should enter the *sanyasi*'s apartments apart from cleaning them — and then too the *sanyasi* should be politely requested to vacate the room and the door must be left open.
25. The only time women should have legitimate association with *sanyasi* is to receive teaching or to offer alms.

26. A young woman should never be engaged as a secretary to a *sanyasi*.
27. If a woman is holding a professional meeting with a *sanyasi* in an office then the door must be kept open at all times.
28. When receiving teaching a woman should never be alone but should be accompanied by others.
29. Nowadays *sanyasi*s do need money in order to function — but all monetary transactions must be open to scrutiny. Do not open a personal bank account for the *sanyasi*. There may be a joint account of the monastery or āśrama or trust with an accountant to oversee all transactions.

Sannyasa Dharma in *Upanishats*

As already mentioned, lot many Upanishats, in lot many places, talk about *Sannyasa*, rules and *dharmas*. In the *Paramahamsa*, the *Brahma*, the Nārada- parivrājaka and the *Sannyasa* Upaniṣats numerous rules are laid down about *Sannyasa*. But the antiquity and the authenticity of these Upaniṣats is extremely doubtful and therefore passing them over, attention will be confined to the Dharma-sūtras and many other *smritis* and Puranas which dilate upon the characteristics and duties of ascetics (*yati-dharma*). Some of the most salient features are set out below with a few references;

1. *Narada Parivraajaka Upanishat* – The ten virtues of asceticism are boldness, patience, humility, lack of stealth, holiness, sensuality, intellect, education, truth and non-anger.

2. <u>*Chandokya Upanishat*</u> – By attaining Brahmam the *Sanyasi* immortality rapidly.

3. <u>*Brahadaaranyaka Upanishat*</u> (II. 4. 1) – we see that *Yajñavalkya* when about to become a *parivrājaka* (a wandering ascetic) tells his wife Maitreyī that he was going to leave home and that he wanted to divide whatever wealth he had between her and her co-wife Kātyāyanī. This shows that a *parivrājaka* had even then to leave home and wife and to give up all belongings.

Again same *upanishat* (II.4.1) – Those who realize ātman give up the hankering after progeny, possessions and heavenly worlds and practice the beggar's mode of life; therefore the brahmin, having completely mastered (and so risen beyond) mere learning, should seek to be like a child (i.e. should not make a parade of his latent capacities or knowledge) and having completed (gone beyond) knowledge and *bālya* (child-like behaviour) he should attain to the position of a *muni* and having risen beyond the stage of a *muni* or non-*muni*, should become a real brahmin (one who has realized *brahmam*).

Again same *upanishat* (III.5.1) – All those who realized the *Atman* (soul) must sacrifice everything – Leaving all lineage, possessions and worldly ties, they seek to live like the life of a beggar; Therefore, *Brahmam*, who has fully mastered the learning (and therefore rises beyond it), must be like a child (i.e. not to do with his hidden abilities or march of knowledge) and knowledge and youth (like child-behavior). He must attain the status of a Muni and must rise beyond the non-Muni level and become a true Brahmam (the one who has fully realized Brahmam).

4. The <u>*Jabālopaniṣat*</u> declares that the ascetic (*parivrāṭ*) wears discoloured (not white) garments, has a tonsured head, has no possessions, is pure, hates (or injures) no one, begs for alms and thereby tends to attain non-difference from Brahmam.

The same *Upanishat* further says – In order to qualify himself for *Sannyasa*, a person had to perform a sacrifice to Prajapati in which whatever he had he distributed to priests and the poor and the helpless.

The *Jabalopaniṣat* adds that the sacrifice should be for Agni (and not for Prajapati as some hold).

Sannyasa Rules – a brief summary

Many rules are thus stated in the Shastras. Those who have attained *Atma-Saakshaatkaara*, those who strive for it, will become the form of Bhagavan. Therefore, their conjecture happens. The wealthy grahastas get all kinds of welfare and benefits by serving them.

Tasmādātmagñam Hyarcayē Būtikāmaḥ |

A summary of the advises of all these texts;

Asceticism is to leave everything and the mind to be pure and mature. Doing karmas and other worldly activities in the previous three ashrams, then leaving them all – Sacrifice karmas and karmic benefits – Only then is one worthy of asceticism.

The *Vedas* are merged in *Gayatri*. Gayatri is sub-merged in the *Pranava* mantra *'Om'*. Fundamentally the *sanyasi* should always chant that *Pranava mantra* daily (24 x 7).

From the point of view of a person belonging to the first three ashrams, the Yati is always in the form of Narayana. He therefore deserves the honor of the Lord.

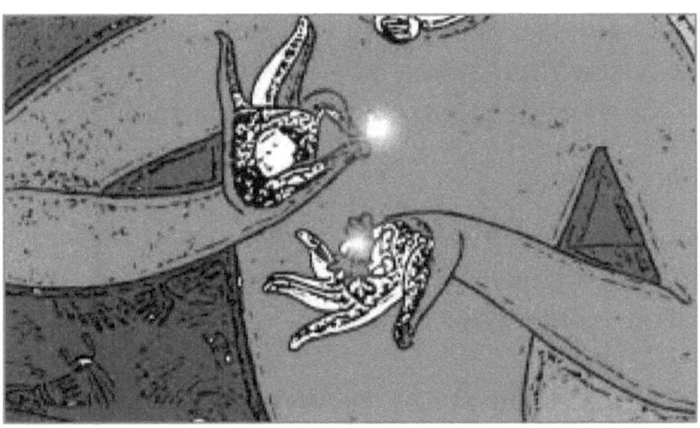

*****

Classes of *Sanyasam*

There are three things prescribed for a monastic *ashramam* – *shravanam* (listening), *mananam* (memorizing – stirring what is heard), and *nididhyasanam* (sacrificing everything).

Lot many texts have divided *Sanyasis ashramam* into four types;

The *Soota-Samhita* (*Maana-Yoga-Kaandam* Chapter 6), *Bikshuko-panishat* and *Prajapati* (as quoted by *Apsararkar*) define these four.

The *Mahabharata* (*Anusāsana Parvam* 141.89) says that ascetics are of four types;

- *Kuṭīcaka,*
- *Bahūdaka,*
- *Haṃsa* and
- *Parama-haṃsa,*

each later one being superior to each preceding one.

The *kuṭīcaka*, as the name itself implies, is one who resorts to *Sannyasa* in his own house or in a but erected by his sons, begs food of his sons and relatives, wears the top-knot, the sacred thread, has the three staffs, carries a water-jar and stays in the same hut.

The *kuṭīcaka* stay in the hermitages of sages like *Gautama*, *Bharadwaj*, *Yajñavalkya* and *Haritha*, take eight morsels of food every day, know the essence of the path of Yoga and hanker only after *moksha* (liberation).

A *sanyasi* may stay in the same hut to listen and memorize – to learn again and again, to study, to get resolve the doubts. Therefore, these stages are called "*kuteechaka* asceticism".

The *bahudakas* have three staffs, the water-jar and wear garments dyed with ochre, beg for food at seven houses of sage-like brahmins or other well-conducted men but avoid taking flesh, salt and stale food.

Bahūtakaḥ Sa Vikñēyaḥ Sarvasaṅgavivarjitaḥ |
Banduvargē Na Bikṣēta Svabhūmou Naiva Samviśēt ||

Both the type of sanyasis, *Kuteecagar* and *Bahoothakar,* should do *Sandhyavanthanam*[15] and *Gayatri Japa* regularly. Must also continue to do the recommended deity worship.

Svādyāyam Cānvaham Kuryāt Sāvitrīm Santyayōrjapēt |
Śikāyagñōpavīti Syāt Dēvatārādanam Carēt |
Dyāyīta Dēvamēkāntē Satatam Paramēśvaram ||

Self-realization is not the main goal of these two. But for a monk it is a state of purification or a compulsory advancement from the previous three monasteries. Thus, not only Veda Vyasa but also *Sri Vidyaranya* has mentioned in his precious work "*Jeevan Mukti Vivekaḥ*". Hence, frustration is only the intensity here. *Devata* worship and *japam* are primarily recommended for these two types. This is made clear by understanding the definition of the three penances propagated by these monks.

The main purpose of these two stages of *sannyasa ashram* is to master the threefold mastery of speech, mind and actions/ body. The procedure for controlling these facilities is specifically described;

Vāgdaṇṭaśca Maṉō Daṇḏō Karmadaṇḏastataiva Ca |
Yasyaitē Niyatā Puddhou Sa Tridaṇḏīti Cōcyatē ||

Mindfulness, depression or altruism of the outside world and *prana* sobriety are the recommended ways. As *Kamalakara* notes describe – *japam* and devotional worship facilitate one or all of these. Again, again, *Savitri* is just japam. There is no other *mantra*.

According to the scriptures, as per the Veda sentence "*Aham Brahmasmi*", those who transcend these *kuteecaka* and *bahoodaka* states are called "*parivraaja sannyasis*". *Parivrajam* means "to wander". They should not stay in one place for more than 3 nights. They have to

[15] The *Sandhyavanthanam* of the monks differs from that of others. Importance is given more to the *Gayatri Mantra*.

travel the across the country and spread the *Sanatana Dharma* and teach the sciences to all. Resolve all doubts and bless the devotees.

3. *Hamsa* – The *haṃsas* stay not more than one night in a village and not more than five nights in a town for alms or subsist on cow's urine or dung, or fast for a month or always perform the *candrāyana* penance. *Pitāmahā* quoted in (*varnāśrama*) states that the *haṃsas* carry only one *daṇḍa*, enter a village only for alms and otherwise stay under a tree or in a cave or on a river bank.

4. *Paramahamsas* – The *Paramahamsas* always stay under a tree or in an uninhabited house or in a burial place and either wear a garment or are naked; they are beyond the pairs of dharma and adharma, truth and falsehood, purity and impurity. They treat all alike, they regard all as the Self, to them a clod of earth or gold is the same and they beg alms from persons of all *varnas*.

The *Jabālopaniṣat* (6) describes the state of *Paramahamsas* at great length. They are sages like Samvartaka, Aruni, Śvetaketu, Durvasas, Ribhu, Nidagha, Jaḍabharata, Dattatreya, Raivataka and so on; they do not exhibit any visible signs of their order or any visible rules of conduct; though they are really not mad they behave like one mad; they go out for alms only for keeping body and soul together; they are unaffected by acquisition or absence (of alms), they have no house but wander about and stay in a temple or on a heap of grass, on an ant-hill, or at the foot of a tree or on a river bank or in a cave, they have attachment for nothing, they are centered in contemplation of the one soul.

According to *Soota-Samhita* it is only *hamsa* and *Paramahamsa* that give up *śikha* and the sacred thread.

The difference between *Hamsa* and *Paramahamsa Sanyasis* is not only the severity of the frustration, but also the motives or attitudes.

Procedural liberation is the benefit of *Hamsa Sanyasi*. At the same time *Jeevan Mukti* is the fruit of *Paramahamsa Sanyasi*. The adjustment for these two is very clear.

Śravaṇātirata: Śuddhō Nididhyācaṉatatparaḥ |
Brahmabāvēṉa Sampūjya Brahmāṇḏamakilam Stitaḥ ||
Ātmatruptaścātmaratiḥ Samalōṣṭāśmakāñcaṉaḥ |
Tatvampatārtabōtācca Viṣṇurūpaḥ Swayam Sadā ||

Earlier itself in the *Dharma Shastra* the rules of *Parasara* and *Paramahamsa Sanyasi* were emphasized.

The *Paramahamsa* should have only one *daṇḍa*. There are two types of *sannyasa dharma*, which are mainly based on the wisdom of the soul wisdom viz.;

Sri Vishnu Bhagavatam (3.12.43) describes of four types of monks – a monk who lives in his hut and observes the rules of the monastery properly is *kuṭīcaka*. A *Bahūdaka* is one who goes on the path of enlightenment without considering karma as important. A *Hamsa* is the recipient of *Gnanayoga Siddhi*. Giving up all efforts one who attains Jeevan Mukti is inactive and is called *Paramahamsa*. Thus the four monastic norms are created.

5. *Vidvat* (those who have already realized *Brahmam*) and
6. *Vividiṣu* (those who are eager seekers after realization) and relies on *Brahadaranyaka Upanishat* (III.5.1)

For the former and *Brahadaranyaka Upanishat* IV.4.22 and *Jabālopaniṣat* for the latter. *Yajñavalkya* is an example of *vidvat-Sanyasa*, which leads to *jivanmuktas* (i.e. release even when the body still persists), while the latter (*vividisā-Sanyasa*) leads to release after the body is no more (i.e. *Videha Mukti*).

"*Sannyasa Shravanam Kuryat*" - According to the Vedic rule of taking *sannyasa* and doing *Vedanta Shravanam*, the sannyasa that accepts for wisdom is "*Vividisha Sannyasa*". Some people do not take *sannyasa*, listen to *Vedanta* and because the wife, son, karmas, etc., are a hindrance to enlightenment *nishtai*, the *sannyasa* that sacrifices and accepts them is "*vidvat sannyasa*".

One who was a *karma sanyasi* can mature and become a *parivrajaka sanyasi*. It is better to progress gradually. Then they can sacrifice the sacred thread and the tuft. Asceticism is itself sacrifice – gradual sacrifice.

Adi Shankara refers to the *Parivrajaka sanyasam* only, who has sacrificed everything. He did not talk about *Eka Dandee, Tri Dandee*, or *Dandee*[16] asceticism itself. Enlightenment *Sannyasa – Adi Shankara* refers to *Parivrajaka Sanyasam*. That is the *Advaita* tradition.

He would carry out his duties from an ashram of pragmatic monks. Instead the heretical monk will wander and perform his duties. He is well versed in *Brahmasamstar – Brahmam*. He does not need all the tools of salvation. The one who has crossed the Samsara ocean – What is the need of the boat?

Sanyasopanishat adds two more types to the four types mentioned above. *Tureeyaateetam* and *Avadhootham*;

7 *Tureeyaateetam* – (Above the 4th stage *Paramahamsa*). Likewise, Cows eat fruits he has to take his food (i.e. he should not hold or store them in his hand). He can only beg from three houses, if he takes the cooked food. He does not wear clothes. Only his body continues to live (but he does not know that fact), he treats his body as if it is dead.

In *Sri Devi Gita* verse (7-34-42), *Sri Devi*, herself explains about *Tureeyaateetam*.

8. *Avadhootam*[17] – The *avadhootar* is beyond all control. He can take food from all races except those who are accused of mortal sins or who are excommunicated (expelled). He should be like *ajakars* (like mountain snakes) – that means lying down and just opening the mouth without any effort. He should be internalized only in thinking about the true nature of *Brahmam*.

---

[16] A separate chapter has been included about *Dandee Sanyasam*.

[17] Separate chapters have been included about *Avadhoota Sanyasam* and the earliest *guru Dattareya*.

Manu (VI.33) asserts – *Avadhoota* asceticism does not mean violating all the rules of science. There is no such thing as do's and don'ts (prescriptions and restrictions) for such monks.

One who was a *karma sanyasi* can mature and become a *parivrajaka sanyasi*. It is better to progress gradually. Then they can sacrifice the sacred thread and the tuft. Asceticism is itself sacrifice – gradual sacrifice.

<u>*Chaturmasya Virata*</u>

The monks usually stay in one place for 4 months only during the *Chaturmasya* fast. This is due to the fact that it is difficult to get out during the rainy season as one has to travel the country on foot, as worms can bite/ disturb the way in the forest.

Nowadays, according to the scripture "*Pakśāvai Māsāḥ*" – 4 *Pakshas* are considered as 4 months and everyone follows up this *virata* for only 2 months.

This *Chaturmasya virata* begins on the full moon day of the month of *Aashaadha* with the Veda *Vyasa* Puja. It is said that during this *Chaturmasya virata* period, performing service, foot worship (*pada puja*), *Biksha Vandanam*, etc. for the monks, the person gets the benefit of performing 1000 *Ashvamedha Yajnas*.

It is not necessary that only after becoming a sage, one has to practice the three states of *Shravanam*, *Mananam* and devotion. Those who have matured beyond the state of hearing and/ or mind before attaining asceticism can reach the third stage directly. Within oneself, the *Gayatri Mantra* is condensed in the *Pranava* of the soul and the *Gayatri Mantra* is in a state of maturity with the *Vyahruti mantras*. When the *Gayatri Mantra* is unable to propagate, the *upasaka* can be placed straight in the third position.

*****

Dandee Sanyasee

Some monks hold a stick in their hand. What is its significance? What is a three-pole? What is the difference between a one-pole and a three-pole? Some monks hold the stick. Some do not keep? A cloth is tied at the end of the pole. What is it? For what? Can it be changed? This chapter is trying to respond to these doubts of an ordinary man.

One thing has to be remembered first – the sage who is holding the *dandam* should be called as "*Dandee Sanyasi*". Some call them as "*danda sanyasi*". In Tamil this gives a wrong meaning.

Kaya, Vaca, Manasa (body, speech and mind) – these are represented by the three – as a symbol of the three *Dandams* (Three-*Dandee*), said to the monks. What the mind thinks, the mouth should speak. The body has to do what the mouth speaks. After such maturity – after going to the state of self-control the three *dandams* can be merged to one - Three *dandams* can be converted into a single *dandam*. The monks who hold the penance are called the *dandee sanyasi*. A *dandam* is inseparable from a monk.

Monks in general can be of two types. *Karma sanyasi* and *Gnana Sanyasi*.

Dandee Sanyasi should perform eternal puja and karmas. Therefore, he is called *Karma Sanyasi*. He does not usually sacrifice *yajnopaveetam* and tuft. He can sacrifice them as he matures and moves on to the next situation.

One *Dandee Sanyasi* can provide *Dandee sanyasam* only to others. One non-*Dandee Sanyasi* cannot provide *Dandee sanyasam* to others.

Kuteechaka and *Bahoodaka sanyasis* should have a *dandam* always. They have to perform daily puja to the *dandams*. Once matured he becomes a *hamsa* or *paramahamsa*, they he can sacrifice the dandam in a river.

The *guru*, who gives sanyasam to the disciple only first hands over the *dandam* to him. He has to keep it safely alongwith the concerned *mantras*.

Generally, a sanyasi has to protect his *Dandam*, very carefully. In case, if it is lost or broken, after doing some prescribed remedies, he can take a new one.

Even at the cost of duplication, various *shastra* sayings about a *dandam* have been summarized below;

According to *Yājnavalkeeyam* (III.58), he should be *tridaṇḍi* (carrying three staffs), while *Manu* (VI.52) simply says he should be *daṇḍi*. The word *daṇḍa* is used in two senses, a staff of bamboo or restraint.

Boudhayana Dharma Sutra (II.10.53) gives an option that he may be *eka-daṇḍi* or a *tri-daṇḍi* and also says that he should not cause harm to creatures by speech, actions and mind.

Manu (XII.10), which is the same as *Dakṣa* (VII.30), declares that that man is called tridaṇḍi who has restraint over his speech, mind and body. *Dakṣa* makes certain apt remarks — Even gods who pre-eminently possess the *sattva-guṇa* are carried away by pleasures of sense; what of men? Therefore, he who has given up his taste for pleasures should resort to *daṇḍa*; others cannot do it as they will be carried away by pleasures.

An ascetic is not called *tridaṇḍi* by carrying bamboo staffs; he is *tridaṇḍi* who has the spiritual *daṇḍa* in him. Many people make their livelihood under the guise of (carrying) three *daṇḍas* (VII.27-31, quoted by Aparaarkar).

Laghu-Viṣṇu (IV.12) says he may be *ekadaṇḍi* or *tridaṇḍi*.

The *Jīvan-mukti-viveka* quotes verses to the effect — he who wields the staff of the knowledge of Reality is called ekadaṇḍi, while he who merely holds a stick in his hand without knowledge and eats everything (or has all sorts of desires) reaches terrible hells.

Vishnu says – *Hamsa sanyasi* can have only the things – one yagnopaveetam, a single *dandam*, a saffron garment, a comfortable garment to move the insects on the earth (for the *ahimsa* purposes). The remaining things are the same as before.

Yagñōpavītam Daṇḍam Ca Vastram Jantu Nivāraṇam |
Tāvat Parigrahaḥ Prōktaḥ Nāṉyō Hamsa Parigrahaḥ ||

Sage *Atri* says – *Paramahamsa sanyasi* can have only two loincloths, a torn-out blanket and a *dandam*.

Bodhaayana says – The *Kuteecaka sanyasi*, after obtaining Sanyasam, should take food in his or his relatives house. He should have tuft, holy thread, three *dandams* and water-pot. He should continue to do *Gayatri japam* regularly.

Angirasa says – A *sanyasi* should have a sacrificial thread and a triple staff (*dandam*).

Pitāmahā quoted in (*varnāśrama*) states that the *haṃsas* carry only one *daṇḍa*

The *Paramahamsa* should have only one *daṇḍa*.

Dasha naami Sampradayam or Tradition refers to the Yogic title of the *Sanyasi*s, who were descended from Adi Shankara tradition, holding one *Dandam* in a hand, to observe the Hindu Religion.

Group of *sanyasi*s belonging to Ramakrishna Mission are also part of the *Sri Adi Shankara* Order. They have the title of Puri. Yet they do not keep the *dandam* in their hands. They consider themselves to be a Paramahamsa sage. Hence, they do not keep the *dandam*. They learn/ study the *Gnana kaandam* of *Vedas*.

The *Sanyasi*s of the *Ramanuja Sampradaya* wear orange-coloured cloth, a holy thread and tuff and Tri-danda or three- staff. At present, they are very few in number.

Bhavishya Puranam says – The qualifications of a *Daṇḍam* is – should be of bamboo, beautiful, leathery, even number knotted, has many a black dot (sign of completion), with no branches, straight, sprouting from the ground, up to the nose/ eyebrows. Such a staff should be worn by the *sanyasi*.

Daṇḍam Tu Vaiṇavam Soumyam Satvacam Samaparvakam |
Puṇya Stāṉasamutpaṉṉam Nāṉākalmāpa Śopitam ||

The *Vāyu Purāṇa* I.8 (quoted by Aparārka) lays down what he should possess. He should take a staff of bamboo the outward surface of which is intact, which is not formidable and which has the parvans (the parts between the joints) of equal length, which is surrounded by a rope of cow's tail hair four aṅgulas in length and has three knots and which he holds in his right hand;

Earlier days, while providing *sanyasam*, the *guru* used to give groin cloth to the disciple. That is kept tied to the *Dandam* as an alternate cloth. It can be changed it if is worn out. *Shastras* do not prescribe anything for it.

In ancient times there were no monks called head of mutts. Nowadays, however, according to the title of the *yoga pattam*, the flag of the monastery is tied to it. Some head of mutts make flags out of metal and hang them on the poles.

*****

Chaitanyas

Those who vow to remain in the *Brahmacharya Ashram* itself till the end are called *Naishtika Brahmachari*.

Earlier days there is no specific rituals for this. After the Virata and Samavartana done by the Guru, the person decides and vows himself to live as a brahmachari during his remaining life. A well-known example is *Bheeshma* in *Mahabharata*.

Those who are immersed in the *Chinmudra* and completely acquainted with the all-known Lord Shiva are said to be *Chaitanyas*.

Nowadays – after the *Dasha nama* uttered by *Adi Shankara* – a small ritual is performed by the Guru for this purpose and the sur-name (*yoga pattam*) *Chaitanyar* is also kept. They do not remove the *yagnopaveetam*. It is necessary that they follow the relevant practices. Some are dressed in white and white, others in yellow and some in saffron – just to show off that they are *Chaitanyas*.

Those who have made the *Naishtika Brahmacharya* vow, will not come to the *Sannyasa Ashram* later. However, some contemporary Chaitanyas are allowed to come to the monastery, if their guru considers them worthy. There is a notion that the *Chaitanya* life is a stage of preparation for asceticism.

*****

Sri Dattareya - The Earliest Guru

Kruta Yugē Bagavān Satyadēvaḥ Trētāyām Datta Ēva Ca ।
Dvāparē Bagavān Vyāsaḥ Kalou Śaṅkaraḥ Swayam ।।

There are totally four eras (*yugs*). For each era one *Jagadguru* (guru – teacher for the whole world) originated.

For the *Kruta* era – *Bhagavan Satyadevar.*
For the *Tretaa* era – *Bhagavan Dattareyar.*
For the *Dvaapara* era – *Bhagavan Vyasar.*
For the *Kali* era – *Bhagavan Shankarar.*

In that angle *Bhagavan Dattareyar* is the Jagadguru for the *Tretaa* era.

At every stage of human life, *Brahmacharya*, Grahastam, *Vana-Prastam* and *Sannyasa* the actual guru is to guide the human being. Take him to the true goal of birth is viz., unity of soul-Brahma. He also guides the man to walk according to the rules of scripture. The great task of Sadguru is to help the man to attain the salvation of. This is the great Guru's philosophy mentioned in shastras "*Na Guroratikam Tattvam* – न गुरोरधिकं तत्त्वं".

To show this Guru's philosophy to the world and to exemplify the qualities of a virtuous Sadgurus to the world and Acharya Maha Purushas who are about to incarnate as Sadgurus to lead the human society on the right path, Sat-Chit-Anandam, the Parabrahmam itself decided to incarnate as Gnana.

The great sage *Atri* was engaged in rigor penance in *Rishyamuga Parvat*. *Atri Maharishi*, is the one who conquers the three evil qualities of lust, anger and greed – without triads – that is why *Atri* (a + tri). *Anasuya* Devi, the wife of such a noble *Maharishi*. *Asuya* means jealousy – *Anasuya* is completely devoid of this jealous.

Delighted by Atri Maharishi's meditation, the trinity (*tri murtis*) asked him what boon he should have – he prayed to bless him with a perfect son. To a sage like Atri Maharishi and to a Maha-Pativrata Siromani like

Goddess Anasuya, how else to bless a perfect son other than a child full of the full features of the trinity? Thus Datta + Athreya (दत्त + आत्रेय) appeared as *Sri Dattatreya* as a sign that the trinity had given themselves to him. The story took place in which Anasuya transformed the trinity we all know into children to show the power, glory and omnipotence of Goddess Pativirata Dharma.

Dattatreya (दत्तात्रेय), Dattā or Dattaguru, is a paradigmatic Sannyasi (monk) and one of the lords of Yoga. In Maharashtra, Andhra Pradesh, Goa, Telangana, Karnataka and Gujarat, he is a syncretic deity, considered to be an avatar of the three Hindu gods Brahma, Vishnu and Shiva, collectively known as Trimurti. In other regions, and some versions of texts such as Garuda Purana, Brahma Purana and Sattva Samhita, he is an avatar of Vishnu.

The incarnation philosophy of Adi-guru Sri Dattatreya Bhagavan is that when the evil qualities of jealousy and hatred are removed (*Anasuyadevi*) + and high penance (*Atri Maharishi*) is combined, one attains the state of *Moksha* (*Bhagavan Sri Dattareya*) of Brahma *Saakshaatkaaram*.

With the three faces of the trinity of *Brahma* + *Vishnu* + *Maheshwaran*, Lord *Sri Dattareyar* realizes that *Parabrahmam* is one and the same through the trinity of *Srishti* + *Stiti* + *Samharam*.

Several *Upanishat*s are dedicated to him, as are texts of the Advaita Vedanta-Yoga tradition in Hinduism. One of the most important texts of Advaita Vedanta, namely Avadhoota Gita (literally, "song of the free") is attributed to Dattatreya. Annual festival in the Hindu calendar month of *Margashirsha* (November/ December) reveres Dattatreya and this is called Datta Jayanti.

His iconography varies regionally. In western Maharashtra and Andhra Pradesh, for example, he is typically shown with three heads and six hands, one head each for Brahma, Vishnu and Shiva, and one pair of hand holding the symbolic items associated with each of these gods: rosary and water pot of Brahma, conch and discus of Vishnu, trident and drum of Shiva. He is typically dressed as a simple monk, situated in a forest or wilderness suggestive of his renunciation of worldly goods and pursuit of a meditative yogi lifestyle. In paintings and some large carvings, he is surrounded by four dogs and a cow, which is a symbolism for the four Vedas and mother earth that nourishes all living beings. In the temples of southern Maharashtra, Varanasi and in the Himalayas, his iconography shows him with one head and two hands with four dogs and a cow.

According to Rigopoulos, in the Nath tradition of Shaivism, Dattatreya is revered as the Adi-Guru (the earliest Teacher) of the Adinatha Sampradaya of the Nathas, the first "Lord of Yoga" with mastery of Tantra (techniques), although most traditions and scholars consider Adi Nath an epithet of Shiva. His pursuit of simple life, kindness to all, sharing of his knowledge and the meaning of life during his travels is reverentially mentioned in the poems by Tukaram, a saint-poet of the Bhakti movement. Over time, Dattatreya has inspired many monastic movements in Shaivism, Vaishnavism and Shaktism, particularly in the Deccan region of India, south India, Gujarat, Rajasthan and Himalayan regions where Shiva tradition has been strong. According to Mallinson, Dattatreya is not the traditional guru of the Nath Sampradaya, he was coopted by the Nath tradition in about the 18th century C.E., as a guru, as a part of Vishnu-Shiva syncretism. This is evidenced by the Marathi text Navanatha Bhakti Sara, states Mallinson, wherein there is syncretic fusion of the Nath Sampradaya with the Mahanubhava sect by identifying nine Naths with nine Narayanas.

The puranic stories of Dattatreya are diverse and vary by region. In the Puranas, he was born in north Indian hermitage to Anusuya and her husband the Vedic sage Atri traditionally credited with making the largest contribution to the Rigveda. They are believed to be lived in Mahur, Nanded District, Maharashtra. Another states his father lived in the western Deccan region. A third claims he was born in Kashmir jungles near the sacred Amarnath Temple. A fourth legend states he was born along with his brothers Durvasa and Chandra, to an unwed mother named Anusuya, after sage Atri saw her bathing, fantasized about her which caused her to become pregnant. In a fifth myth, sage Atri was very old when young Anusuya married him and they sought the help of the Trimurti gods for a child. As the trinity were pleased with them for having brought light and knowledge to the world, instantly granted the boon, which led Dattatreya to be born with characteristics of all three.

While his origins are unclear, stories about his life are clearer. He is described in the Mahabharata as an exceptional Rishi (sage) with extraordinary insights and knowledge, who is adored and raised to a Guru and an Avatar of Vishnu in the Puranas. Dattatreya is stated in these texts to having renounced the world and leaving his home at an early age to lead a monastic life. One myth claims he meditated immersed in water for a long time, another has him wandering from childhood and the young Dattatreya footprints have been preserved on a lonely peak at Girnar (Junagadh, Gujarat) and Dattatray make a tapa for 12,000 years over there. The Tripura-rahasya refers to the disciple *Parashurama* finding Dattatreya meditating on Gandhamadana mountain.

Dattatreya is said to have his lunch daily by taking alms at a holy place Pithapuram, Andhra Pradesh, where he was born as Sripada Sri Vallabha (his first avatar).

Self-education – The 24 Gurus of Dattatreya

The young Dattatreya is famous in the Hindu texts as the one who started with nothing and without teachers, yet reached self-awareness by observing nature during his Sannyasi wanderings, and treating these natural observations as his twenty-four teachers. This legend has been emblematic in the Hindu belief, particularly among artists and Yogis, that ideas, teachings and practices come from all sources, that self-effort is a means to learning. The 24 teachers of Dattatreya are:

The 24 teachers from nature

#	Guru	Observation	*Dattatreya's* Learning
1.	Earth	Steadfastly productive, does its dharma, gets abused, heals and is steady in giving nourishment.	Forbearance, remain undisturbed even if oppressed, keep healing even if others injure you

#	Guru	Observation	*Dattatreya's* Learning
2.	Wind	Passes through everything and everyone, unchanged, unattached, like Truth; sometimes becomes a gale, disturbs and changes the world, like Truth.	Be free like the wind, yet resolute true to your own force
3.	Sky	The highest has no boundaries, no limits, is unaffected even if clouds and thunderstorms come and go	The highest within oneself, the atman (self, soul) has no limits, it is undifferentiated non-dual no matter what, let the clouds of materiality pass, be one with your soul and the universal self
4.	Water	Serves all without pride, discrimination; is transparent to everyone; purifies and gives life to everyone it touches	A saint discriminates against no one and is never arrogant, lets other give him impurity, yet he always remains pure and cleanses
5.	Fire	Purifies and reforms everything it comes in contact with, its energy shapes things	The heat of knowledge reforms everything it comes in contact with, to shape oneself one needs the energy of learning
6.	Moon	Waxes and wanes but its oneness doesn't change	Birth, death, rebirth and the cycle of existence does not change the oneness of soul, like moon it is a continuous eternal reality

#	Guru	Observation	*Dattatreya's* Learning
7.	Sun	Source of light and gives its gift to all creatures as a sense of duty; in rain puddles it reflects and seems like distinct in each puddle, yet it is the same one Sun	The soul may appear different in different bodies, yet everyone is connected and the soul is same in all; like Sun, one must share one's gifts as a sense of duty
8.	Pigeons	They suffer losses in the hands of violent hunters, warn against obsessive attachments to anyone or to material things in this world	Do not be obsessive, don't focus on transient things such as damage or personal loss, human life is a rare privilege to learn, discover one's soul and reach moksha
9.	Python	Eats whatever comes its way, makes the most from what it consumes	Be content with what you have, make the most from life's gifts
10.	Bumblebee	Active, works hard to build and create its reserve by directly visiting the flowers, but is selective and uses discretion, harmonious with flowers and never kills or over consumes	Be active, go directly to the sources of knowledge, seek wisdom from all sources but choose the nectar, be gentle, live harmoniously and leave others or other ideologies alone when you must
11.	Beekeeper	Profits from honeybees	Don't crave for material pleasures or in piling up treasures, neither the body nor material wealth ever lasts
12.	Hawk	Picks up a large chunk of food, but other birds harass him, when it drops its food other birds leave him alone	Take what you need, not more

#	Guru	Observation	*Dattatreya's* Learning
13.	Ocean	Lucid at the surface, but deep and undisturbed within; receives numerous rivers yet remains the same	Let rivers of sensory input not bother who you are deep inside, know your depths, seek self-knowledge, be unperturbed by life, equipoise
14.	Moth	Is deceived by its senses, it runs to the fire in misunderstanding which kills it	Question your senses, question what others are telling you, question what you see, know senses can deceive, seek reason
15.	Elephant	Is deceived by his lust, runs after the smell of a possible mate, and falls into a pit made by mahout's then fettered and used	Don't lust after something or someone, don't fall into traps of others or of sensory gratification
16.	Deer	Is deceived by his fear, by hunters who beat drums and scare him into a waiting net	Fear not the noise, and do not succumb to pressure others design for you
17.	Fish	Is deceived by bait and so lured to its death	Greed not the crumbs someone places before you, there are plenty of healthy opportunities everywhere
18.	Courtesan	Exchanges transient pleasure with body, but feels dejected with meaningless life, ultimately moves on	Many prostitutes their time, self-respect and principles for various reasons but feel dejected with their career and circumstances, seek meaning and spirituality in life, move on to doing things you love to do

#	Guru	Observation	*Dattatreya's* Learning
19.	Child	Lives a life of innocent bliss	Be a child, curious, innocent, blissful
20.	Maiden	She is poor yet tries her best to feed her family and guest, as she cooks, she avoids attracting attention to her kitchen and poverty, by breaking all her bangles except one on each wrist	Don't seek attention, a yogi accomplishes and shares more through solitude
21.	Snake	Lives in whatever hole that comes his way, willingly leaves bad skin and molts	A yogi can live in any place, must be ready to molt old ideas and body for rebirth of his spirit
22.	Arrowsmith	The best one was so lost in his work that he failed to notice the king's procession that passed his way	Concentrate on what you love to do, intense concentration is the way to self-realization
23.	Spider	Builds a beautiful web, destroys and abandons the web, then restarts again	Don't get entangled by your own web, be ready to abandon it, go with your atman
24.	Caterpillar	Starts out closed in a tiny nest but ultimately becomes a butterfly	Long journeys start small, a disciple starts out as insignificant but ultimately becomes a spiritual master

The appearance of Shri Dattatreya in pictures varies according to traditional beliefs. A typical icon for *Dattatreya*, particularly popular with Marathi-speaking people in India, has three heads corresponding to *Brahma-Vishnu-Shiva*, and six hands; the lowest two hands carry rosary (*mala*) and water pot (*kamandalu*), middle pair of hands hold hourglass mini-drum (*damaru*) and trident (*trisula*), and top two hands have conch (*shankh*) and spinning wheel (*chakra*).

Many older medieval temples of Dattatreya show him with just one head, such as the one in Mahur, one at Narayanpur on Pune Satara Road, Near Pune, and another in Pandharpur, both in southern Maharashtra. Texts such as Agni Purana describe the architectural features for building murti, and for Dattatreya, it recommends him with one head and two hands. In Varanasi, Nepal, north Himalayan foothill states of India, 15th century C.E., Nath temples of Dattatreya show him with just one face. In western parts of Maharashtra, the syncretic six armed and three faced iconographies is more common.

He is the motif of the '"honey bee" Yogin who has realized advaita knowledge. Dattatreya as the archetypal model of syncretism.

Furthermore, the unfolding of the Dattātreya icon illustrates the development of Yoga as a synthetic and inclusive body of ideologies and practices. Although fundamentally a jñāna-mūrti, Dattātreya is a "honey bee" Yogin: one whose character and teachings are developed by gathering varieties of Yoga's flowers. For all religious groups whose propensity it is to include ideas, practices, and teaching from the ocean of traditions, Dattātreya is truly a paradigm.

Another distinctive aspect of Dattatreya iconography is that it includes four dogs and a cow. The four dogs represent the Vedas,[4] as trustworthy all-weather friends, company and guardians, while the cow is a metaphor for mother earth who silently and always provides nourishment.

Alternate iconography - Dattatreya's sculptures with alternate iconography have been identified in 1st millennium C.E., cave temples and archaeological sites related to Hinduism. For example, in the Badami temple (Karnataka), Dattatreya is shown to be with single head and four hands like Vishnu, but seated in a serene Yoga posture (padmasana). Carved with him are the emblems (lañchana) of the Trimurti, namely the swan of Brahma, the Garuda of Vishnu and the Nandi of Shiva. The right earlobe jewelry and hair decoration in this art work of Dattatreya is of Shiva, but on his left the details are those of Vishnu. Rigopoulos dates this Badami sculpture to be from the 10th to 12th century C.E.

A sculpture similar to Badami, but with some differences, has been discovered in Ajmer (Rajasthan). The Ajmer art work is a free statue where Dattatreya is standing, has one head and four hands. In his various hands, he carries a Trisula of Shiva, a Chakra of Vishnu, a Kamandalu of Brahma, and a rosary common to all three. Like the Badami relief work, the Ajmer iconography of Dattatreya shows the swan of Brahma, the Garuda of Vishnu and the Nandi of Shiva carved on the pedestal with him.

The historic Indian literature has interpreted the representation of Dattatreya symbolically. His three heads are symbols of the Gunas (qualities in Samkhya school of Hinduism). The three Gunas are Sattva, Rajas and Tamas. The six hands have ethical symbolism, namely Yama, Niyama, Sama, Dama, Daya and Shanti (axiology in Yoga and Vedanta school of Hinduism).

The Kamadhenu cow is symbolic Panchabutas, the four dogs are inner forces of a human being: Iccha, Vasana, Asha and Trishna. In these interpretations, Dattatreya is that yogi Guru (teacher) who has perfected all these, rules them rather than is ruled by them, and is thus the Guru Dattatreya is beyond them.

Texts

The Dattatreya *Upanishat* (tantra-focused), Darshana *Upanishat* (yoga-focused) and particularly the *Avadhoota Upanishat* (advaita-focused) present the philosophy of the Dattatreya tradition. Dattatreya is also mentioned in the classic text on Yoga, the Shandilya *Upanishat*.

Other *Upanishat*s where Dattatreya's name appears in lists of ancient Hindu monks revered for their insights on renunciation are Jabala *Upanishat*, Narada Parivrajaka *Upanishat*, Bhikshuka *Upanishat* and Yajnavalkya *Upanishat*. Of these, his mention in the Jabala *Upanishat* is chronologically significant because this ancient text is dated to have been complete between the 3rd century B.C.E. and 3rd century C.E.

Dattatreya is mentioned in the Mahabharata and the Ramayana.

Dattatreya is mentioned in the ancient chapter 9 of the Sattva Samhita and chapter 5 of the Ahirbudhnya Samhita, both among the oldest layer of texts in the Vaishnava Agama tradition (Panca-ratra). Schrader states these texts and the chronology of Dattatreya are older than the Mahabharata, but Rigopoulos disagrees with him on the chronology.

In the Hindu tradition, Dattatreya is the author of Avadhoota Gita, or the "Song of the free". The text's poetry is based on the principles of Advaita Vedanta, one of the sub-schools of Hindu philosophy.

The extant manuscripts have been dated to approximately the 9th or 10th century C.E., but it may have existed earlier as part of an oral tradition. It consists of 289 shlokas (metered verses), divided into eight chapters.

Many Mahatmas received advice from Adi-guru Datta, who was traveling as a sage and a great yogi. The most important disciples are – *Parashuramar, Prahlathan, Karthaveeryarjunan*, Sri Karthikeyan, Sage Sankruti and so on.

Let us all consider *Dattareya* as our Guru in our mind and take his blessings.

*****

Avadhoota Sanyasam

अद्वैत गुरु परंपरा स्तोत्रम्

नारायणं पद्मभुवं वशिष्ठं शक्तिं च तत्पुत्रं पराशरं च व्यासं
शुकं गौडपादं महान्तं गोविन्दयोगीन्द्रं अथास्य शिष्यम् ।
श्री शंकराचार्यं अथास्य पद्मपादं च हस्तामलकं च शिष्यम्
तं तोटकं वार्त्तिककारमन्यान् अस्मद् गुरून् सन्ततमानतोऽस्मि ॥

Advaita Guru Paramparā Stōtram

Nārāyaṇam Padmabuvam Vaśiṣṭam Śaktim Ca Tatputram Parāśaram Ca Vyāsam Śukam Gouḏapātam Mahāntam Gōvindayōgīntram Atāsya Śiṣyam |
Śrī Śaṅkarācāryam Atāsya Padmapādam Ca Hastāmalakam Ca Śiṣyam
Tam Tōṭakam Vārttikakāramaṉyāṉ Asmat Gurūṉ Santatamāṉatōśmi ||

Greetings to the Guru dynasty – from *Narayanan* to *Brahma* to *Vasishta* – from *Sri Shankaracharya* to his disciples *Sureshwarar, Padmapada, Hastamalakar, Todagar* and the followers of this *Guru* dynasty – *Namaskarams* to all.

There are 17 Upanishats relating to *Sanyasam*. Below is a list of them;

#	Veda	Upanishat
1.	*Rig*	*Nirvāṇam*
2.	*Krishna Yajur Veda*	*Avadhūtam*
3.		*Gata Rudram*
4.		*Brahmam*
5.	*Shukla Yajur Veda*	*Jāpālam*
6.		*Turīyātītam*
7.		*Paramahamsam*
8.		*Bikśukam*
9.		*Yajgavalkyam*
10.		*Cātyāyaṇi*
11.	*Sāma Veda*	*Āruṇeyam*
12.		*Kuṇtikam*

#	Veda	Upanishat
13.		*Maitreyā*
14.		*Sanyāsam*
15.		*Nārada Parivrājakam*
16.	*Atharva Veda*	*Parabrahmam*
17.		*Paramahamsa Parivrājakam*

All these Upanishats elaborate on the rules and regulations of the *Sannyasa Ashram*. They also outline what to do and what not to do – prescriptions and restrictions.

Among these, the *Nirvana Upanishat* of the Rig Veda and the *Avadhoota* Upanishat of the Krishna Yajurveda speak volumes about the *Avadhoota Sannyasa Ashram*.

The *Upanishats* clarify the six stages of monastic life, explained in another chapter above;

1. *Kuteechagar* – Ashram resident
2. *Bahoothakar* – Supported by many
3. *Hamsar* – Hamsa bird
4. *Paramahamsar* – The great Hamsa bird
5. *Tureeyaatheetar* – Fourth – Beyond the bonds of nature
6. *Avadhootar* – Free from all worldly connections and debts

The *Avadhoota Ashram* is not a separate ashram like the four ashrams mentioned earlier. It is the last stage inside the *Sannyasa ashram*. That is the means of salvation.

The *Sannyāsopaniṣat* and defines *'avadhūta'*— The *avadhūta* is beyond all restrictions, he takes food from all varnas except those who are charged with mortal sins or are *patita* (outcasts) and eats like an *ajagara* (a boat constructor) i.e. lying down and opening only his mouth without any effort and is solely absorbed in the contemplation of the real nature of the Spirit. Medhātithi (on *Manu* VI. 33) is quite emphatic that *Sannyasa* does not consist in defying all the rules of śāstra, but in giving up the sentiment of egoism and of possessiveness and that it is not true to say that for the *sanyasi* all rules (even of morality) are non-existent.

The *avadhoota* monks will first be the *'dhoota'* monks. For *dhoota* monks there is no dress code. After they mature, they become an *avadhoota* monk. Then for them the sky is the roof, the earth is the house and the directions are the dress (i.e. no clothing). *Yateşţam – Yetaḥ Işţaḥ – Anu-Vikramya – Yatecchayaḥ* – Without desire – Food available automatically.

At the end of this period, all the cosmic powers of the sage are united. They are now flowing in his strong and raging current. He is no longer a tributary flowing towards the source, but rather a main stream flowing straight into the sea. He is integrated with the source. He has attained enough individuality to live and function as an enlightened soul in the world.

He places himself in one place and allows the disciples to come around. At this point he is free to start his own work or do what he thinks is most beneficial. He can choose anything – it belongs to him.

The final stages of the asceticism cannot really be described. Because they are in a world of inefficient levels of highest consciousness. *Avadhootam* means a fully realized *Jivanmukta*, (liberated soul), to the extent that every one of its duties has been fulfilled.

Avadhoota monks do not always cut their hair and nails. They have no obligations such as holding a *Dandam* or so. Some, however, observe the *Chathur Masya Viratam* – as is the custom of their *gurus*.

Lord Sri Dattareyar[18], in the essence of all his teachings, blessed the traditional religion of *Avadhoota*. *Avadhoota Ashram* is a state of being that benefits from the maturity of the fully enlightened. The sciences say that this is the fifth highest monastery beyond the *Sannyasa Ashram* and that it is a special state called *Avadhoota Charyai*.

---

[18] There is one another chapter about Lord *Dattareyar*.

Many people have different opinions and criticisms about the *sadhus* who have resorted to asceticism. Under the guise of *sadhu,* some people are engaging in illegal activities – not only illegal under the constitution of the country – but also illegal the laws imposed on the *shastras*. They could be around 1% of the total number of *sadhus*. The remaining 99% are real *Sadhus – Swamijis* – representatives of the Gods – the lords cannot speak directly to us. That is why there are such representatives as *Swamijis*. One should have done virtues of earlier births before joining or being in contact with them. Also need the blessings of ancestors. Let us touch the feet of all of them and bow down so that we may live a life of rapture.

*****

Miscellaneous *Sanyasis*

Rishikesh and Haridwar are colonies for *Sanyas*is in India. Varanasi also is among the chief abodes of *Sanyas*is.

1. *Shaivas* – In South India, there are Tamil *Sanyas*is who belong to the Kovilur Mutt, Thiruvavaduthurai, Dharmapuram Adheenams and so on. They do not belong to the *Sri Shankara* order. They are also called Shaivas – *Veera Shaivas*. Usually they wear a lingam engraved medal around their neck.

2. *Naagas* – Nagas are Shaiva *Sanyas*is. They are usually in a naked state. They smear their bodies with ashes. They have beard and matted locks.

3. *Udasis* – Guru Nanak's order of ascetics are called *Udasis*. They correspond to *Sanyas*is and *Vairagis*. They are indifferent to the sensual pleasures of this world (*Udasina*). Hence, they are called *Udasis*.

4. *Vairaagis* - A *Vairagi* is one who is devoid of passion. Vairagis are *Vaishnavas*. They worship Lord Rama, Sita and Hanuman. They read Ramayana of Tulsidas. The mendicant Vaishnavas of the Ramanandi class are the Vairagis. This ascetic order was instituted by Sri Ananda, the twelfth disciple of Ramananda.

5. *Rama Sanehis* – The founder of this order was Ramcharan who was born in the year 1718 in a village near Jaipur in Rajasthan. The Rama Sanehi mendicants are of two classes, viz., the *Videhis* (literal meaning foreigner) who are naked and the *Mohinis* who wear two pieces of cotton cloth dyed red in ochre. Their monastery is in Shahapur in Rajasthan. The Rama Sanehi sect has the largest following in Mewar and Alwar. They are found also in Bombay, Gujarat, Surat, Poona, Ahmedabad, Hyderabad and Varanasi.

6. *Kabir Panthis* – Kabir Panthis are the followers of saint Kabir. They are numerous in all the provinces of Upper and Central India. There are twelve branches. Kabir Chaura is at Varanasi. It is a big monastery of Kabir Panthis. Dharamdas was the chief disciple of Kabir. The followers

are expected to have implicit devotion to the Gurus, in thought, word and deed. They should practice truthfulness, mercy, non-injury and seclusion. The followers of Kamal, son of Kabir, practice Yoga.

7. *Dadu Panthis* – The Dadu Panthis form one of the Vaishnava cults. Dadu, the founder of this sect, was a disciple of one of the Kabir Panthi teachers. The followers worship the Lord Rama.

Dadu was a cotton cleaner. He was born at Ahmedabad. He flourished about the year 1600. The Dadu Panthis are of three classes, viz., the Viraktas who are bareheaded and have one cloth and one water-pot, the Nagas who carry arms and who are regarded as soldiers and the Vistar Dharis who do the avocations of ordinary life.

The Dadu Panthis are numerous in Marwar and Ajmer. Their chief place of worship is at Naraina, which is near Sambhur and Jaipur. Passages from the Kabir writings are inserted in their religious scriptures.

8. *Gorakhnath Panthis* – Gorakhnath was a contemporary of Kabir. He is regarded as the incarnation of Lord Siva. He calls himself as the son of Matsyendranath and grandson of Adinatha. There is a temple of Gorakhnath at Gorakhpur in Uttar Pradesh. Bhartrihari was a disciple of Gorakhnath.

The followers of Gorakhnath are usually called Kanphatas, because their ears are bored and rings are inserted in them, at the time of their initiation. They worship the Lord Siva.

9. *Nimbarka Sampradayis* – There are Sadhus of the Nimbarka Sampradaya. There are Vaishnavas.

10. *Ramanuja Sampradayis* – The *Sanyas*is of the *Ramanuja Sampradaya* wear orange-coloured cloth, a holy thread and tuff and Tri-danda or three- staff. At present, they are very few in number. They are also called as *Jīyar* — They follow the *Vishishtadvaita* tradition. Most of the zealots went from grahastaashrama to asceticism. There are some exceptions – very few moves to *sannyasa* directly from the *Brahmacharya Ashram*. They normally do not sacrifice *Yajnopaveeta*.

Although the text refers specifically to males, *Ramanuja* himself initiated 300 female ascetics. Nowadays many Hindu monastic orders admit women so all the rules and regulations apply equally to members of both genders.

11. *Parinami Sect* – Sri Pirannath is the founder of this sect. He was born in 1675 at Jamnagar, district Rajkot, in Kathiawar. He was the Divan of Raja Jam Jasa. The followers are to practice Ahimsa, Satya and Daya—non-violence, truthfulness and compassion. They study the sacred book, Kul Jam Swarup, or Atma-Bodha, in Hindi, which contains the teachings of Sri Pirannath. It contains 18,000 Chaupais. They worship Bala-Krishna, i.e., Krishna as a small lad.

The followers are found mostly in the Punjab, Gujarat, Assam, Nepal and Bombay. There are two Mutts or monasteries—one at Jamnagar and the other at Pamna.

12. *Akhada Sanyasis* – They are of two types viz., *Niranjani Akhada* and *Jhuna Akhada* – They belong to the order of *Sri Sankara*. They are also *Dashanamis*. They are found in the Uttar Pradesh State only.

13. *Nrupati Parivrajaka* — *Parivrajaka* means a wandering monk, mendicant, an anchorite. In the Gupta period inscriptions, there are several records of a line of kings who were the landlords of the imperial Guptas and held the title of "*Nrupati-Parivrajakar*" (royal monks).

They belong to the Bharadwaj Gotra and are said to be the incarnation of founder Kapil. After they became a king, they eventually became monks. And his disciples (in the style poetically described by Kalidas) became monks after adorning the throne for some time. Hence, they were called Nrupati-Parivrajakas.

14. *Sadhu* — same as a parivrajaka or wandering ascetic.

15. *Yati* — literally "a striver" a synonym for a monk.

16. *Bhikṣu* — a "requester of alms" — can be applied to both Hindu and Buddhist monks (*bhikkhus*).

17. *Swamiji* — is only a formal title of address, it does not refer to the avocation of a renunciate.

18. *Aabat Sanyasis* – (Sanyasam taken in emergency) When a person is very sick, dying, he can opt for *Sannyasa* without even going through elaborate processes.

Daksha Says;

Āturāṇām Ca Saṉyāsē Na Vidirṉaiva Ca Kriyā |
Praiṣamātram Samuccārya Saṉyāsam Tatra Pūrayēt ||

The *Jabālopaniṣat* (5) allows *Sannyasa* to those even who are suffering from illness and are about to die, all that is required being that they should declare in words and resolve in their mind to enter the order of *Sannyasa*. No extensive ceremonial is required.

Angiras and *Sumantu* state — When a person is shattered by old age or harassed by his enemies or is suffering from (an incurable) disease he may resort to *Sannyasa* by merely uttering the *praiśa* and no further rites would be absolutely necessary. He should recite thrice in the morning, at noon and in the evening— "I have given up everything (or entered upon *Sannyasa*)" and further say I forswear whatever action I may have done through ignorance, indolence or carelessness; I shall cause no harm to creatures with my hands or feet, with my speech, body or mind; may all creatures have no fear from me.

The Dharma-Sindhu (III, uttarārdha) says that in this sannyasa for those at the door of death the absolutely essential elements are the resolve (*sankalpa*), the uttering of the *praiśa* and the giving of the promise of non-injury and the rest of the rites may or may not be performed according to circumstances.

Even now such a *Sannyasa* (called *ātura-Sanyasa*) is sometimes resorted to by religious-minded men *in extremis*, the only essentials gone through being *sankalpa* (declaration of resolve), *kṣaura* (tonsure of the head), *savitrī-praveśa* and *praiśa-ucāra* (utterance of *praiśa*).

*****

Some Questions Answered

Some generic doubts discussed in the form of Frequently Asked Questions - FAQs.

1. Is it that only Brahmins can take up Sanyasam or others also?

This has been discussed and answered earlier also. However, it is repeated.

One important question on which opinion was sharply divided is whether *Sannyasa* was allowed to all the three varṇas or only to Brahmins. Let us refer some shastra evidences in this regard;

'This Self brahmins seek to know by the study of the Veda'; *Brahadaaranyaka Upanishat* IV.4.22 states — After knowing this Self, brahmins give up the hankering after progeny, wealth and heavenly worlds and practice begging.

Brahadaaranyaka Upanishat III.5.1 continues – Closely examining the worlds that are the rewards of actions, a brahmin should come to be disgusted etc.

Mundaka Upanishat I.2.12 – Closely examining the worlds that are the rewards of actions, a brahmin should come to be disgusted etc.

Here, the word *'brahmin'* being used, śruti indicates that brahmins alone can be *sanyasi*s.

Manu (VI. 38) begins his description of the 4th stage with the words — 'a brahmin should leave his house and go into the world as a wanderer' and winds up the chapter (VI.97) by saying — I have declared this fourfold procedure in relation to brahmins.

The *Jabālopaniṣat* ordains — whether a man has fulfilled his *vratas-*

samavartanas[19] or not, whether he has performed *samavartana* (the ceremonial bath after studying *Vedas*) or not, whether his fires (Vedic) have ceased or not he should resort to the wandering ascetic's life the very day on which he feels disgust with mundane affairs.

It thus allows even a *brahmacari* to become an ascetic; a *kṣatriya* and *vaiśya* could also be a *brahmacari*. *Yājnavalkeeyam* (III.32) states that *Sannyasa* is a means of purification (of the mind) in the case of twice-born classes. Besides the only condition precedent mentioned by the Jabālopaniṣat for resorting to *pravrājya* (ascetic life) is *vairagya* and whoever feels the latter is authorized to betake himself to that stage.

Yājnavalkeeyam (III.61) while laying down the observances of ascetics employs the word *'dvijaḥ'* and not *'brāhmanaḥ'*.

Both these opposing views are supported by the most famous authors. The first view that only brahmins can be *sanyasi*s is affirmed by the great *Shankaracharya* in his *Bhashyam* for *Brahadaranyaka Upanishat* III.5.1 and IV.5.15. It is most interesting and also very refreshing that *Sureshvara* in his *Vārtika* on *Śaṅkara's Bhashyam* on *Brahadaranyaka Upanishat* III.5.1 first explains the views of his *guru*, then enters the lists against his great master and combats his views with cogent arguments. Most of the medieval writers and works such as *Medhātithi* on *Manu* (VI.97), the *Smrtui-muktā-phala* uphold the view that only brahmins can resort to the 4th *āśrama*, while a few works like the *Smruti-candrika* support the second view.

So far as the smriti texts and the medieval works are concerned a śūdra could not become a *sanyasi*. The Shanti-parva (63.11-14) is quite dear that a *śūdra* cannot be a *bhikṣu*. It also (18.32) informs us that in its day many (probably including śūdras) assumed the outward signs of the 4th *āśrama*, got their heads tonsured and moved about in ochre-coloured garments (*kāśāya*) for securing alms and gifts. But there are clear indications that śūdras did assume even in the times of

19 Guru performs *Upanayanam* to the student and takes him to Gurukulam for studies. After teaching all the 4 Vedas he performs 4 Vratas (graduation ceremonies) Samaavartanam is a part of it.

ancient smṛtis the ascetic's garb and mode of life. When the *Āśrama-vāsika-parva* 26.33 states that Vidura was buried as an ascetic, the commentator Nīlakaṇṭha remarks that this indicates that even śūdras can follow the mode of the ascetic life.

2. Can ladies also take sanyasam?

This has also been answered earlier.

When the question is asked whether *sūdras* or women could resort to *Sannyasa* there is likely to be some confusion. The word *'Sannyasa'* conveys two ideas:

(a) Relinquishing of all actions (*kāmya karma*) that spring from the desire to secure some object or other and secondly,
(b) Following a certain mode of life (*āśrama*) the outward signs of which are carrying a staff and the like and the entrance into which is preceded by the utterance of the *praiṣa*.

The *Jīvan-mukti-viveka* states that *moksha* (*amṛtatva*) depends upon *tyāga* (abandonment) as stated in the *Kaivalyopaniṣat* (2) — "not by actions, nor by progeny nor by wealth, but by tyāga some attained *moksha*" (liberation) For such abandonment even women and śūdras are eligible!

The best example of a woman giving up everything being that of *Maitreyī*, the wife of *Yājñavalkya*, who plainly told the sage (Brahadaranyaka Upanishat IV.5.3-4) — "What have I to do with that which will not make me immortal (will not release me from samara)?"

The *Bhagavad-gīta* (18.2) also declares that *Sannyasa* means the giving up of actions springing from desires (to secure certain objects).

The *Jīvan-mukti-viveka* further states that by resorting to the āśrama of *Sannyasa* the mother and the wife of a *sanyasi* are supposed not to be born again as women (but they may be born as men). Hence women and *śūdras* may renounce all actions, though they could not adopt the peculiar ascetic mode of life with its outward symbols. According to Sankara's Bhashyam on *Vedānta-sūtra* (I.3.34) the order of *Sannyasa*, the peculiar rules of which are recommended by Vedic texts, is only for the three varṇas, while the practice of mere nyāsa (relinquishing of worldly pleasures and desires) can be resorted to by women, *śūdras* and mixed castes.

It appears that even women could in rare cases adopt the ascetic's life in ancient Brahminic times. The Maitreyar on Yājnavalkeeyam III.58 quotes a *sūtra* of *Baudayanam*, (*strinām caike*) to the effect that according to some ācāryas even women could adopt the ascetic mode of life.

Patañjali in his *Mahābhāṣya* speaks of a woman ascetic (*parivrājaka*) named *Śaṅkarā*.

In the drama called *Mālavikāgnimitra*, *Kalidāsa* describes the *Paṇḍitā Kausikī* as wearing the garb of an ascetic (I.14).

It must be said that the general trend of Hinduism is against women adopting the homeless or ascetic life. One important reason for the same is ladies and the fourth class do not *upanayanam* and do not wear have *yagnopaveetam*. No *agni karmas* also. They have nothing to sacrifice. When nothing is prescribed for them, what is there to sacrifice.

Present day sanyasis, mostly, follow the sannyasa principles of *Sureshwaracharya* – most importantly in North India. Since the ladies and fourth class have nothing to sacrifice, they cannot take formal sannyasa rituals and hence no sanyasam based on *Shastras*. However, if they a matured mind and *vairagya* there is no objection for them to lead an ascetic life. As a symbol of this they can have a dress of different colour and probably a different name also. They can also aim at liberation or reaching *brahmam*. They can perform pujas to lord of their wish. Best example will be Sharada Devi wife of Ramakrishna Paramahamsar.

3. Sannyasa for physically challenged;

Some teachers on the other hand say that one may depart for the mendicant's life immediately after completing study. Some teachers also recommend that the blind and handicapped should also renounce early. If a person has chronic ailment or is facing an imminent death then he too may renounce.

Some espoused the view that *Sannyasa* was meant only for the blind, the cripple and the impotent, that is, for persons who possessed no eligibility (*adhikāra*) for the performance of Vedic rites.

Shankaracharya in his Bhashyam on Vishnu Sahasranamam (III.4.20) refutes the view that the passage of the *Jabālopaniṣat* cited above relates to those who are not eligible for performing Vedic rites and establishes that that passage has in view the general prescription that there is a stage of life called *parivrājya* (*Sannyasa*) meant for all that seek release from *samsara*.

Medhatithi on *Manu* VI.36 rejects this view (of some) by saying that the blind or cripple cannot follow the rules and practices (such as not staying in one village for more than one night) just as they cannot perform Vedic rites and hence it could not have been intended by the smriti writers that *Sannyasa* was only for the blind and the cripple, nor can the impotent take to *Sannyasa* as no upanayana is performed in their case.

4. Can a person after becoming a Sanyasi return to the previous ashrama?

One of the principal rules for a yati was that he was to leave wife and home and never to think of sexual matters or to revert to the life of a house-holder.

Sage *Atri* (VIII. 16 and 18) declares — I see no penance (expiation) for that twice-born man, who, after having resorted to the duties of a celibate (*sanyasi*), reverts from that stage; he is neither a *dvija* nor a *śūdra*, his children become caṇḍālas called *Vidura*.

Śaṅkara on Vishnu Sahasranama (III.4.42) explains that these words are only intended to emphasize the great effort required to remain celibate as a *sanyasi* and that expiations are as a matter of fact prescribed for a bhikṣu having sexual intercourse. Dakṣa VII. 33 requires the king to brand on the forehead with the mark of a dog's paw and banish from the kingdom a person who after becoming a *sanyasi* does not abide by its rules (of celibacy etc.). It has been seen above that a man who falls away from the order of *sanyasi*s became a slave of the king for life.

Dakshan (VII.33) says – After becoming a monk if he does not follow its rules, the king must brand him on the forehead with the mark of a dog's foot and expel him from the kingdom. A man who deviates from the rules of the monks becomes a slave to the king for the rest of his life.

If a *sanyasi* continues to engage in sexual activity he will be born as a beetle living in dung for 60,000 years. Thereafter he will be born as a mouse living in abandoned houses. And then he will be reborn as a dog for 12 lifetimes, then he will become a vulture for 20 years and a pig for 9 years (*Shatapata Brahmanam* and *Vayu Puranam – Yati Dharma Sangraham)*.

5. Some people continue to wear yagnopaveetam and tuft even after sanyasam.

One question on which controversies have raged from very ancient times is whether an ascetic should give up his topknot and sacred thread also.

The Jabālopaniṣat (5) states that *Atri* asked *Yajñavalkya* how a man who did not wear a yajñopavīta (when he became an ascetic) could still be a brahmin and that the great sage replied that in the case of the ascetic the Self was his yajñopavīta.

The same Upaniṣat (6) states that the paramahamsa is to abandon in water the three daṇḍas, the water-jar, the śikha, the begging bowl, the water-strainer, the topknot and yajñopavīta and should be a seeker after the Self.

In the Arunika Upanishat (i) it is said that he should discharge his yajñopavīta on the earth or in water and that he should give up his śikha and the sacred thread.

Śaṅkara in his Bhashyam on Brahadaranyaka Upanishat (III.5.1) sets out at some length the arguments and the authorities on both sides and ultimately gives it as his own view that the sacred thread and śikha should be given up by the ascetic.

On the other hand, Vṛddha-Harīta (VIII.57) declares — If an ascetic gives up the acts peculiar to brahmanas, viz. keeping a topknot and wearing a sacred thread, he becomes a caṇḍāla while alive and is born a dog after death.

In modern times *Sanyasis* of the Advaita school give up these two whereas the Vaishnavas do not.

6. Some sanyasis perform *Chaturmasya Vrata* and some do not. Still they have the same yoga pattas like *Giri*, *Saraswathi* and all.

The rule for a *Parivrajaka Sanyasi* is that he has to continuously wander around the country. During rainy season he can stay in one place for 4 months and that is *Chaturmasya Vrata*.

When a sanyasi already stays in a single place, where is the question of *Chaturmasya Vrata* for 4 months. Hence, they do not perform *Chaturmasya Vrata*.

It all depends on the practice of their *gurus*.

7. Some people take sanyasam twice. Is this possible?

A person taking a sanyasam is a new birth – *punar janma*. Already self-*pindam* has been offered for the person and *pinda-samyojanam* has been performed for the previous *ashrama* as if he is dead. How can he take sanyasam again? Can a person have *upanayanam* twice? In the same manner there is no question of twice *sanyasam*.

8. What should be done when a *sanyasi* attains *moksha*? Is *Sraddha*, *Aradhana* and all applicable to him? Can it be performed by son of the previous *ashrama*? Will this be different in the case of *Aabat Sanyasam*?

As already mentioned, a person taking a sanyasam is a new birth – *punar janma*. Already self-*pindam* has been offered for the person and *pinda-samyojanam* has been performed for the previous *ashrama* as if he is dead. That is, the body born in this world is treated as dead already and necessary *samskarams* have been performed by self.

Only his soul is alive upon asceticism. No rites are mentioned anywhere in the *shruti* or *smriti* for his body after *Siddhi*. Just as a mark of respect the body is buried with Vedic mantras or hymns like Vishnu Sahasranama. During the burial, arch leaves and vibudhi are placed in the tomb. It is customary to place the body in water or soil without any ritual. It used to be customary to leave the body in the flowing river. To prevent water pollution, burying in the soil is more common nowadays.

It is also customary to cut the body of an *avadhoota* monk into 8 or 16 pieces and throw them in water or soil.

In traditions, there are some minor variations between south and north of India.

A monk should always be doing *Pranava Japa*. Mainly he knows the final period of his body. Then *Pranava Japam* without any other action should be focused on one, his *Agna Chakra* (between the two eyebrows). In doing so his prana will pass through the any of the nine holes of the body, whichever hole was most used.

For a *Jeevan Mukhtar*, his *prana* has to go through the *Sushumna Nadi*, upwards, through the *Moortha* (apex skull), breaking the skull. This is possible only for a *yogi*. Since this does not happen nowadays, it is customary to break a coconut on the top of the skull before placing the body in the tomb. This has been named as *Kabala Moksham*.

A monk is called a 'refugee'. That means there is no *gati*. Among the five primary elements water and earth are the standard. That is why the body of a dead monk is disposed of in either of these two ways. No rituals are prescribed.

Some monks sit in *Nirvikalpa Samadhi*.

- If he comes out from there by himself, he will be called *'Varan'*.
- If he is summoned out by others he will be called *'Varīyan'*.
- If he does not come out at all he will be called *'Varişţan'*.

If he did not come out for 21 days, he would be considered as having attained *moksha*. They are called *Jeevan muktas*. He is said to have become a *Jeeva samadhi. Nerur Sadashiva Brahmendra*, who showed the people all these three stages, is a good example of this.

Aabat sanyasam is nothing different from other normal sanyasam, excepting that a person who is seriously sick takes this type of sanyasam. Hence all the rules applicable to normal sanyasis are valid for them also.

After the taking the asceticism of a sage, the question of the *shraddha* done by the *poorvashrama* son not arise. He has already performed self-*sraddham*. He has no son, no brother, no wife.

Nowadays it is customary to perform an *Aradhana* for a monk on the day of his passing. *Teertha Narayana* Puja is performed and meals are served to 16 *Vaideekas*. According to *Shodasha Kala Purusha* – the root of the soul has 16 *kalas* – accordingly 16 sages have to be fed. It is not right to dine the *grahastas* like this. *Keshavaadhi*[20] 12, *Guru, Parama guru, Parameshti guru, Paraapara Guru* – a total of 16.

9. Can a couple take sanyasam together? Can they live as a couple even after taking sanyasam?

---

[20] *Keshavaadhi* 12 – *Keshava, Narayana, Madhava, Govinda, Vishnu, Madhusoodana, Trivikrama, Vamana, Shreedhara, Rishikesha, Padmanabha* and *Damodara*.

It has earlier been said that no proper Vedic asceticism is prescribed for women. Therefore, the question of whether the couple can take sanyasam together does not arise.

After the couple leaves for *vanaprastha*, a few years later, the husband matures and decides to accept asceticism. Then the wife should be sent to her son. After that he has to look at his wife, son or other relatives as strangers.

10. Can one monk bow to other monks?

It has been discussed that sanyasam is a re-birth. Hence the age of a monk has to be calculated from the date of sanyasam. In this angle, a junior sanyasi in age can bow to other senior (in age) sanyasis. This is irrespective of the age from the original birth.

*****

Other Books of the Author

http://ramamurthy.jaagruti.co.in/

#	Title	Remarks	Pages
		Indology Related	
1.	*Shrī Lalitā Sahasranāmam*	English translation of Shrī *Bhāskararāya's Bhāśyam*	750
2.	Power of *Shrī Vidyā*	The secrets demystified – with lucid English rendering and commentaries	80
3.	*Samatā*	An exposition of Similarities in *Lalitā Sahasranāma* with *Soundaryalaharī*, *Saptaśatī*, *Viśṇu Sahasranāma* and *Shrīmad Bhagavad Gīta*	172
4.	*Advaita* in *Shākta*	Advaita Philosophy discussed in Shakta related Books	80
5.	*Shrī Lalitā Triśatī*	300 divine names of the celestial Mother – **English** translation of *Shrī Ādhi Śaṅkara*'s *Bhāśyam*	193
6.	Secrets of *Mahāśakti*	Chandi demystified	78
7.	*Daśa Mahā Vidyā*	Ten cosmic forms of the Divine mother	60
8.	ஸ்ரீவித்யா பே ங்கள்	ஸ்ரீவித்யா உபாசனையின் படிகள் - கோவை ஶதச் சண்டீ மலர்	51
9.	ஸ்ரீ ே வீ ஸ்துதிகள்	பல முக்கிய அம்பாள் ஸ்தோத்ரங்கள்	133
10.	Śrī Devī Stutis – श्री देवी स्तुतिः	Various important stotras of Sri Devi	223
11.	ஷண்மத மந்த்ரங்கள் - षण्मत मन्त्राः	பொள்ளாச்சி ஸ்ரீ ஸஹஸ்ரசண்டீ மஹாயாக நினைவு மலர்	145
12.	*Śanmata Mantras* - - षण्मत मन्त्राः	Important Mantras relating to Gods of six religions	87
13.	தேவதா மந்த்ரங்கள்	அக்கரைப்பட்டி ஸஹஸ்ரசண்டீ மஹாயாக நினைவு மலர்	32
14.	ஆதி ஶங்கரரும் ஷண்மதமும்	ஷண்மதங்களைப் பற்றிய ஒரு அறிமுகம்	32
15.	ஸ்ரீ ஷண்மத தேவதா அர்ச்சனை	ஸ்ரீ மஹா கும்பாபிஷேக மலர்	64
16.	*Vaidhīka* Wedding	Typical Wedding process in English	56
17.	வைதீகத் திருமணம்	Typical Wedding process in Tamil	57
18.	ஸ்ரீ லலிதா திரிஶதி	300 divine names of the celestial Mother – Tamil translation of Shrī Ādi *Śaṅkara*'s Bhāśyam	234
19.	ஸ்ரீகுரு பா பூஜா வி ானம்	சித்தகிரி ஸஹஸ்ரசண்டீ மலர்	44
20.	ஸ்ரீவித்யா ஶடாம்னாய மந்த்ரங்கள்	சித்தகிரி ஸஹஸ்ரசண்டீ மலர்	60
21.	*Ekatā*	Oneness among Shiva, Vishnu and Shakti	277
22.	*Vedas* – An Analytical Perspective	A description of Veda, Vedanta, Vedanga, Jyotisha, Shastra, etc.	240
23.	*Shrīvidya* Variances	Variances in Srividya Upasana	50
24.	வே ங்கள் – ஒரு பகுப்பாய்வு	A description of Veda, Vedanta, Vedanga, Jyotisha, Shastra, etc.	280

#	Title	Remarks	Pages
25.	பரமாச்சார்யாள் நோக்கில் ஸ்ரீலலிதாம்பிகா	The explanation given by Paramacharya on some of the names in Lalita Sahasranama	175
26.	*Ṣaṇṇavati* (षण्णवति *Tarpaṇa*	Repaying Debts to Ancestors	42
27.	ஷண்ணவதி (षण्णवति தர்பணம்	முன்னோர் கடன் தீர்த்தல்	48
28.	*Shrī Mahā Pratyangirā Devī*	Holy Divine mother in ferocious form	41
29.	ஸ்ரீ மஹா ப்ரத்யங்கிரா தே வீ	தெய்வீக அன்னையின் பயங்கர வடிவம்	51
30.	*Śrī Chakra Navāvarṇam*	Marvels of *Śrī Chakra*	115
31.	ஸ்ரீ சக்ர நவாவர்ணம்	ஸ்ரீ சக்ரத்தின் அதிசயங்கள்	130
32.	அம்பிகையின் (திரு) அவதாரங்கள்	ஸ்ரீ தேவியின் பல்வேறு அவதாரங்கள்	142
33.	Incarnations of Holy Mother	Different Incarnations of *Śrī Devī*	140
34.	ஸ்ரீ பிரணவானந்தர் - ஒரு சரிதம்	ஒரு அரிய ஸ்வாமிகளின் திவ்ய சரிதம்	91
35.	ஸன்யாஸம் - ஓர் அலசல்	ஹிந்து மத ஸன்யாஸ பேதங்கள் - ஒரு பகுப்பாய்வு	140
36.	Asceticism – an Analysis	A Study of Hindu *Sanyasam*	140
37.	ஶாந்தமும் ப்ரணவமும்	(ஸ்ரீ ஶாந்தானந்தரும் ஸ்ரீ ப்ரணவானந்தரும்) குரு சிஷ்யருக்கு உபதேசங்கள்	120
38.	ஶாக்த உபநிஷதங்கள்	ஸ்ரீ தேவியைப் பற்றிய உபநிஷதங்கள்	400
39.	*Shakta Upanishats*	*Upanishats* about *Sri Devi*	83
Applied Samskrutam Based			
40.	*Paribhāshā Stora*-s	An exploration of *Lalitā Sahasranāmam*	96
41.	*Shrī Cakra*, An Esoteric Approach	Mathematical Construction to draw *Shrī Cakra*	64
42.	Number System in Samskrutam	An overview of Mathematics based on Samskrutam	123
43.	*Vedic* Mathematics	30 formulae elucidated	146
44.	Vedic IT	Information Technology and Samskrutam	162
IT Based			
45.	Orthogonal Array	A Statistical Tool for Software Testing	180
Banking Based			
46.	Retail Banking	A guide book for Novice	213
47.	Corporate Banking	A guide book for Novice	232
48.	Dictionary of Financial Terms	A Guide Book for all – Demystifying Myriad Global Financial Terms	215
49.	GRC in BFS Industry	(**G**overnance, **R**isk Management and **CO**mpliance by Banking & Finance Industry)	200

Let him be blessed to share his knowledge and experience with others through more books. Let us wish him all the best.

*****

Bibliography

The following books were referred to write this book. Lot many thanks to the authors and the publishers. They were very useful.

#	Title of the book	Author
1.	यतिकर्म-परिचय	श्री स्वामी शांताश्रम जी महाराज्
2.	ஸங்க்ஷேப தர்ம ஶாஸ்த்ரம்	மஞ்சக்குடி வெங்கட்ராம சாஸ்த்ரிகள்
3.	The Hindu Monastic Code	U. Ve. Sri Rama Ra*manu*ja Achari
4.	ஈசாவாஸ்ய உபநிஷத்	ஶ்ரீ ஸ்வாமி பரமஹம்ஸானந்த ஸரஸ்வதி
5.	यतिधर्म प्रदीपिका	श्री श्री श्री सच्चिदानन्दतीर्थ महास्वामि
6.	Other books of the same author.	

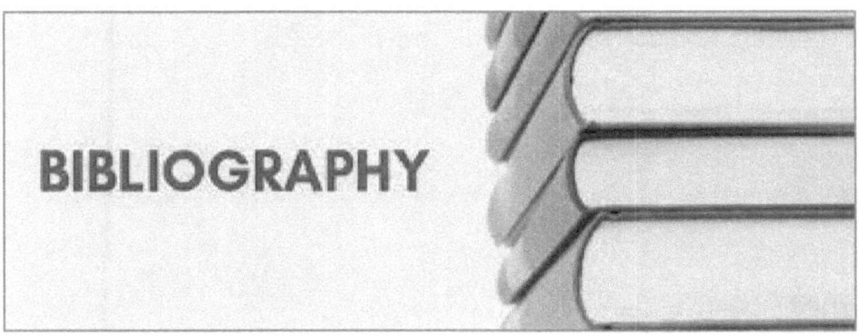

Om Tat Sat ॐ तत् सत्

*****

www.ingramcontent.com/pod-product-compliance
Lightning Source LLC
Chambersburg PA
CBHW050018170726
48282CB00025B/457
* 9 7 8 9 3 8 2 2 3 7 6 7 9 *